VLADIM

HOST
THE
HOLY
GHOST

FOREWORD BY DAVID DIGA HERNÁNDEZ

ISBN: 978-1-951201-27-2 (Paperback)

978-1-951201-28-9 (Hardcover)

Printed in the United States of America

Table of Contents

Vlad Savchuk is an emerging voice in this generation. He not only operates in the power of God but walks in a realm of purity and humility that is very rare these days. In his new book, *Host the Holy Ghost,* he shares how his understanding and friendship with the Holy Spirit transformed his life and marriage and impacted his ministry and church. I highly recommend this revelatory book to Christians everywhere. The author is not just one who speaks the truth but is a practitioner of the gospel of Jesus Christ and friend of the Holy Spirit.

— **Jeremiah Johnson**
Apostolic Leader of the Ark Fellowship
Best-selling Author of *The Power of Consecration*
www.jeremiahjohnson.tv

Pastor Vlad is a frontlines general raising a global army of kingdom citizens. In his new book *Host the Holy Ghost,* he brilliantly describes our desperate need as Christians to fellowship with the Holy Spirit! We cannot afford to live beyond or outside of God's presence. This writing will fuel your faith for radical Spirit-filled living.

— **Ryan LeStrange**
Founder and Apostolic Leader of TRIBE International
Network of Ministries
Author of *Breaking Curses, Overcoming Spiritual Attack* and
Supernatural Access & more
www.ryanlestrange.com

Through his personal experiences and revelations from the Scriptures, Pastor Vlad helps us to discover how to get to know the Holy Spirit as a Person and develop a deeper relationship with Him. To know the Holy Spirit as your friend is life's greatest treasure, and this book will encourage and inspire you to seek His friendship above all others. I pray that as you read *Host the Holy Ghost,* you will experience the depths of God's love being poured upon your heart by the Holy Spirit and for His love to captivate your heart forever!

— **Andres Bisonni**
International Evangelist
Author of *My Beloved Holy Spirit*
www.holyspirit.tv

Foreword

*T*he precious Holy Spirit, the very same Who hovered above the face of the deep when the Father spoke all things into existence, comes to forever abide with us the very moment we receive God's gift of salvation. The Holy Spirit gave breath to the beginning, skills to the crafters of the tabernacle items, dream interpretations to Joseph, wisdom to Solomon, psalms to David, a revelation to the prophets, and power unto the early church. The same Spirit Who was in them dwells in you. What's more, the exciting reality is that He can be known. More than a force or a feeling, the Holy Spirit can be a Friend. You can learn what it is to walk in freedom, power, holiness, and fellowship with the Holy Spirit as you grow in your understanding and surrender to Him.

As a believer, you have been given the high privilege and the pure joy of being a host of the Holy Spirit's presence. That truth, among many core concepts regarding the nature and power of the Holy Spirit, is what my friend Vlad Savchuk explores in this anointed work, *Host the Holy Ghost*.

Vlad Savchuk is one of the most recognizable and influential figures within a new wave of this generation's Christian leaders who are effectively leveraging modern means of communication while remaining faithful to the gospel message. Pastor Vlad has been blessed with many gifts a strong teaching grace among them. He has an unusual ability to take lofty concepts and present them in a succinct and memorable manner. I often refer to his short and insightful quips as "Vladisms."

Host the Holy Ghost is a gem-filled work in which you will find truths that carry the potential to revolutionize everything about your Christian walk. As you read, many of your questions about the Holy Spirit will be answered, and your spiritual hunger will intensify to the point that your heart will cry, "Welcome, Holy Spirit!"

Aside from the gospel message, I consider friendship with the Holy Spirit my core ministry message and introducing the Holy Spirit as a divine assignment. My desire is to see this generation come to know the Holy Spirit in a profound way. That is why I was so excited to learn about this great resource. That's also why I encourage you to read this book. Believer, I encourage you to read this and often revisit the truths upon which it expounds. Pastors and leaders, allow me to humbly suggest this as a small group or leadership curriculum.

Thank you, Pastor Vlad, for making this available. May all who read this book step into a greater awareness of and a deeper appreciation for the abiding presence of the precious Holy Spirit.

David Diga Hernandez
Evangelist, Healing Minister, TV host
Author of *Carriers of the Glory*
www.davidhernandezministries.com

A Crippled Christian

I grew up in a conservative Pentecostal church in the country of Ukraine. That is where I first learned about the Holy Spirit and speaking in tongues. Even though I'd heard a lot of preaching on the topic of the Holy Spirit, He was still a mystery to me. In fact, most of the time, I referred to Him as "It": like a force, a wind, or a supernatural power. I did not view the Holy Spirit as a Person. He was more like a good feeling, an atmosphere, a power, or a physical tingling experience that I felt whenever my favorite song was being sung and my emotions were stirred.

At the age of thirteen, my family moved to the United States. Some years later when I married my wife, I noticed how differently she related to the Holy Spirit. Her conversations with me made me realize I didn't know the Holy Spirit as a Person. Every time she described to me how God encountered her, she would use phrases like, "Holy Spirit came to me," "Holy Spirit spoke to me," or "Holy Spirit visited me." She didn't refer to Him casually; the Holy Spirit seemed to be a real Person to her. It was always as though she was talking about her close Friend. But for me, whenever I described an encounter with God, I referred to it as the "presence" of the Lord, the "power" of God, or the "anointing" of God.

It never occurred to me to mention the Holy Spirit by His name. Even though I often preached about the Holy Spirit, I did not perceive Him as a real Person. I remember that at a certain moment, I promised myself that I would start to attribute my experiences in God's presence to the Person of the Holy Spirit. I did that for about two weeks, and then again, I forgot and switched back to my old perception of Him. The Holy Spirit was my forgotten God—the God I did not know personally.

Looking back, I can compare myself—and anyone else who doesn't know the Holy Spirit personally—to the crippled man in Acts 3.

> *And a certain man lame from his mother's womb was carried, whom they laid daily at the gate of the temple which is called Beautiful, to ask alms from those who entered the temple; who, seeing Peter and John about to go into the temple, asked for alms.*
>
> **(Acts 3:2-3)**

I could relate to this man. No, I wasn't born physically lame, but this man's physical condition was a picture of my spiritual dilemma. He was born lame from his mother's womb. He was carried to the temple and laid there to beg for money. But one day, Peter and John met him and, instead of giving him money, they gave him something even more valuable that changed his entire life.

This lame man had legs at birth, but those legs didn't work. He couldn't walk. Let me emphasize: he was born with legs, but he lived his life not using them; he crawled and had to be carried by others. His problem wasn't that he didn't have legs; his legs just didn't support him. We have legs, not just to have them on our bodies, but so they can carry us wherever we want to go. His legs didn't carry him; instead, he carried them.

Since the fall of Adam, everyone, at their natural birth, gets a "gift" from the devil—a sinful nature. However, because of Jesus Christ's death on the cross, our heavenly Father gives us a precious gift upon our new birth—the Holy Spirit. His Spirit is given to us at the moment of our conversion, our new spiritual birth, which we call salvation. When we are reborn, we actually invite the Holy Spirit to come into our lives to take over. We submit to Him and our lives are changed—we are born again! The Holy Spirit doesn't come as an upgrade a year later or only after our water baptism. And contrary to popular Pentecostal belief, the Holy Spirit doesn't come to live in us when we begin speaking in tongues. He's not a reward for reaching a certain level in our spiritual maturity. He is ours, and He lives in us from the moment that we are born again!

Let's go back to the lame man. Just as he got legs at birth, so it is with us; we receive the Holy Spirit at our spiritual rebirth. None of us walked out of our mother's womb. We had to learn how to use our legs and to walk. Some take longer than others to learn. In other words, legs come with birth, but walking comes with practice. Legs are a gift, but walking is an action. Your birth was a relatively quick event, but learning to walk took time. As for the lame man in the book of Acts, unfortunately, he had a physical disability and had to crawl and depend on others to carry him.

This was a prototype of my relationship with the Holy Spirit, and I think it's probably the same for many Christians. I had the Holy Spirit in my heart, just as this lame man had legs on his body, but I didn't know the Holy Spirit as a personal Friend. Even though I had Him, I didn't walk and talk with Him. My spiritual life and ministry felt more like crawling in the flesh than boldly walking in the Spirit. I was a crippled Christian.

Paul urges believers who already have the Holy Spirit to *"walk in the Spirit"* (Galatians 5:16). All Christians have the Holy Spirit, but not all Christians walk in Him. So many of us are like this lame man:

- We have legs but don't walk.
- Legs are present but they don't carry us.
- Legs are present but we are brought to the temple by others.
- Legs are present but we sit at the gate instead of entering.
- Legs are present but we beg for things that are secondary.
- Legs are present but we lie on the ground.

We have the Holy Spirit, but we don't always live a life that is surrendered to Him. It can become normal to live a carnal life according to the flesh. We complain, bemoan our fate, and question our destiny. Why do we carry the weight of our marriages, ministries, and finances all alone, even though we have the Spirit of God living in us? We have the Holy Spirit abiding in us, but instead, we seek and rely on others for solutions.

So many people remain at the gateway to a beautiful breakthrough but fail to enter through it. Their prayer life is nothing more than chasing after things that God has promised them, but they don't see results. Their spiritual life can be characterized by lying in self-contentment instead of walking in God's Spirit, standing in God's Word, and sitting in the finished work of Christ as described in Psalm 1. They don't bear lasting spiritual fruit because of all the busyness and distractions in their lives. This pretty well describes the lame Christian: one whose life is summarized by his ability to operate only in the natural realm. There is very little "supernatural" in his life—his achievements are the result of his own efforts. A lame believer doesn't deny the Holy Spirit, but he lives his life without relying on Him, and therefore, results are minimal. In this scenario, the Christian life becomes hard and, at times, very boring.

We, as believers, weren't meant to carry the weight of life and its many responsibilities all alone. The Holy Spirit dwells in us to help us stay in touch with God through our prayer life and ministry. He wants to alleviate the weight of the load. If we don't walk in the Spirit, we will operate in the flesh. We will toil in the flesh. We will run and grow tired. We will walk and grow weary. We will become bitter and worn out. If we don't learn to walk in harmony with the Holy Spirit, the Christian life will become a difficult yoke and ministry will become a heavy burden.

The lame man in the Bible was sitting and begging instead of leaping and praising. He asked for alms, but what he really needed was healing. Peter and John did not give him money to help him. Instead, Peter took the man's hand and lifted him up—through the power of God—and the man started to walk. Praise God! But even though he could walk, his financial situation remained the same. In fact, his outside circumstances didn't change, yet he started to rejoice and praise God, and then he entered the temple. This miracle led many spectators to put their faith in Christ.

Oh how I could relate to this man! I was a lame leader sitting at the gate, begging God for "alms." The alms that I was chasing were miracles and Holy Spirit power. I thought they would change everything in my life and ministry. I remember begging one person, who was greatly used by God, to pray for me so that I would have power in my life. He looked at me intently and declared, "I can't give you power. You don't need power. You just need to know the Holy Spirit personally and He will release His power." In other words, we don't need alms (miracles, manifestations, power)—we just need to walk in the power of the One we already have abiding in us. We need to get well-acquainted with the Holy Spirit—not just learning more about Him, but knowing Him personally as a Friend. The truth is, we can never get more of the Holy Spirit, or a greater measure of the Holy Spirit, simply because He is an individual Person—we already have Him in all His fullness. But we can and must endeavor to get to know Him personally, more and more on a daily basis, by spending more time talking with Him and loving Him, living in harmony with Him, and listening for His quiet voice speaking into our spirits.

That's what started to happen to me. I turned my prayer from "God, give me Your power" to "Holy Spirit, I want to know You better." The kind of prayer you pray reveals a lot about your understanding of God and yourself. In the parable of the Prodigal Son, the youngest son demanded, "Give me what is mine," and that led him away from his father. But after he was desperately broken, his prayer changed to, "Make me your servant" (Luke 15:11-32). We must change our request and ask for what matters most. Asking for alms is a temporary solution for a crippled life. The lame man needed to get the miracle of walking, not the miracle of money. Yes, we do need revival in our churches, but what we need even more is for people to fall in love with the Holy Spirit. We desperately plead for miracles, signs, and wonders, but what we really need is the Person of the Holy Spirit to be noticed, honored, and glorified in our lives.

Slowly but surely, my spiritual life went from crawling and stumbling to walking together with my personal Friend, the Holy Spirit. Maybe I'm not running or soaring in the Spirit yet, but He has become more real to me than ever before. He is no longer a force, but my best Friend. He is no longer just a power, but a real Person.

During one conference, Andres Bisonni[1], whom I highly respect and honor, whispered as he was praying for me, "The Holy Spirit is calling you His friend." I didn't know Andres personally at that time, but only from his YouTube videos. The words from this man of God, who later became my friend, solidified my relationship with the Holy Spirit. It was so pleasant to hear that the Holy Spirit calls me His friend.

Please hear my heart throughout this book. I am not an expert on the Holy Spirit, nor am I some kind of super-amazing author. However, since the Holy Spirit has become a real Person to me, I've seen more miracles, salvations, and deliverances than ever before through the ministry that the Lord has entrusted to me. At Hungry Generation, we now see healings more frequently. Now, at every service, someone gives their life to Jesus, in contrast to before, when we went for two years without a water baptism and nearly six months without seeing anyone get saved. Miracles are not the goal; salvation is. On a personal note, I even noticed a change in my own character, as my wife will testify. But most importantly, the Holy Spirit has become a real and precious Friend to me.

Maybe you are sitting at your temple gate right now, really seeking the power of God or some extraordinary change in your life and

---

1   Andres Bisonni is a traveling evangelist and missionary from South America, and author of *My Beloved Holy Spirit*. More information can be found at holyspirit.tv

ministry. I don't have any hidden secrets to offer you. Silver and gold I don't have, but what I do have, I will share with you. I would like you to switch your focus from the power of God to the presence of the Holy Spirit. He is already in you. Now you need to walk in close harmony with the Spirit, always keeping your focus on Him alone. That walk with Him will change your life and ministry forever. Just as John and Peter lent a hand to a lame person, today in this book, God will use me to lend you a hand to help you get up and walk in the Spirit. Peter and John didn't give the lame man legs; they just activated something he already had.

I can't give you the Holy Spirit. Jesus already did that. But God can use this book to activate a closer relationship with Him, whet your appetite for deep fellowship with Him, and increase your hunger for the Person of the Holy Spirit in your life. An intimate relationship with Him will open up the heavens to you and your ministry. Alms are what you might have desired, but what you actually need is to get up and walk with Him. That's the greatest gift—to know Him and to have a deep, full, ongoing relationship with Him—to "host the Holy Ghost."

In the first chapter, we will look at the foundation of our relationship with the Holy Spirit. It is important to note that He is known by both "Holy Spirit" and "Holy Ghost." "Holy Spirit" is the more common reference, as it is used in the more modern Bible translations. "Holy Ghost" appears in the King James Version of the Bible, which, for many years, was the most widely accepted English translation from the original Hebrew and Greek manuscripts. The terms are interchangeable, and both refer to the third Person of the Trinity. Open your heart and dive into this book. I believe the Lord will use this truth to set you free and set you on fire for Him.

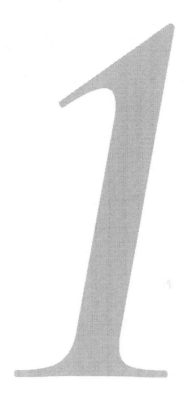

The Dove Descends

The Coming of the Holy Spirit

Chapter 1

The earth was without form, and void; and darkness was on the face of the deep. And the Spirit of God was hovering over the face of the waters.

(Genesis 1:2)

*I*n this chapter, I want to lay a firm foundation for a relationship with the Holy Spirit. This foundation is Jesus! The Holy Spirit will build everything upon this foundation. Before you learn how to have a relationship with the Holy Spirit, you must have a true relationship with Jesus Christ as your personal Savior. A minimal, religious acquaintance with Jesus is not sufficient. When Jesus becomes your foundation, you will begin your exciting journey with the Holy Spirit.

Let's suppose I want to pursue a relationship with the president of the United States. It is not enough to fervently desire to gain that relationship with him. I could go on a hunger strike, protest, or stand in front of the White House with hopes that he would notice me. I could send him many letters and emails and stalk his every move. But all that would do is probably result in my arrest, not a relationship. However, the president's son doesn't have to do any of that. His father initiates the relationship based on the fact that he is his son. The president's kinship with his son lays the foundation for his son's close relationship with him.

Let me state it another way: the kinship that the Holy Spirit already has with you is the foundation of your relationship with Him. Have you ever wondered why the Holy Spirit wants to have a relationship with you? Because of your prayer, fasting, and sacrifices? Perhaps because you evangelize or are in full-time ministry? Not at all! The Holy Spirit's relationship with you is based on Jesus, period. Not on your hunger, humility, or holiness. Jesus is the foundation for the Spirit's relationship with you.

Before we were saved, the Holy Spirit was with us, wanting to reveal Jesus to us. But the Holy Spirit begins His work in us only after we accept Jesus. He comes to live inside of us to develop godly character. He makes us more like Jesus and teaches us the pathways of righteous living. Yes, it all starts with Jesus, the Light, the Word of God!

The Spirit Wasn't yet Given Because Jesus Wasn't yet Glorified

In Jesus' time, during the Feast of Tabernacles, a priest would take a golden vessel to the pool of Siloam early every morning and fill it with clear water from the spring. He would bring it back to the altar with sounds of joyful shouts of acclamation and praises from the people. The crowd would recite a special prayer from the book of Psalms as the pure water was poured out on the west side of the altar. This ritual was a commemoration of the water that God supplied from the rock for the children of Israel during their wilderness wanderings.

Interestingly, this ritual would be repeated for only seven days but not performed on the eighth day, which was the final day of the feast. It was on the final day of the feast that Jesus cried out, *"If anyone thirsts, let him come to Me and drink"* (John 7:37-38). On that day, when no water was brought from the pool of Siloam, Jesus Himself offered rivers of living water to the people.

> *He spoke concerning the Spirit, whom those believing in Him would receive; for the Holy Spirit was not yet given, because Jesus was not yet glorified.*
>
> **(John 7:39)**

And to this very day, Jesus promises us rivers of living water, not a new religion.

All the Jewish feasts, ceremonies, and sabbaths that were established in the Old Testament were just a shadow of things to come, but Jesus is the actual meaning of them all (Colossians 2:16-17). Jesus is the reality behind the ritual of the Feast of Tabernacles. He is the Rock that Israel drank from (1 Corinthians 10:4). Think back to when Moses hit the rock—water came out (Exodus 17:5-6). The same thing happened with our Savior; when Jesus was crucified, water and blood came out of His side when a Roman soldier pierced Him with a spear (John 19:34). This became a significant picture of cleansing by the blood of Jesus and by the water of the Holy Spirit.

As the second-century apologist Tertullian said, "If Adam was a figure of Christ, the sleep of Adam was the death of Christ who was to fall asleep in death; that in the injury of His side might be figured the Church, the true mother of the living."[2] Even as the death of Jesus

---

2   De Anima, XLIII, 10: CSEL 20, 372.

was like the sleep of Adam, it resulted in the birth of the church, just as Adam's bride, Eve, was created from his side while he slept. But more than that, because of Christ's death, the Holy Spirit was poured out upon all believers.

The apostle John said that the Holy Spirit hadn't been given because Jesus had not yet been glorified (John 7:39). "Glorified" in this text speaks of Jesus' death, burial, resurrection, and ascension into heaven. The Father waited for the Son to finish His work of atonement on the cross before sending His Spirit upon the believers. The manifestations of the Spirit came only after Christ was glorified and seated at the Father's right hand in heaven. Pentecost followed the cross. Jesus' death, burial, and resurrection is the basic foundation for the Spirit-filled life. Everyone who wants to walk in the fullness of the Holy Spirit must build upon the foundation of Jesus' glorification.

I remember participating in a winter retreat in the country of Vietnam. It was one of those camp meetings where things didn't start well. Due to a very heavy snowfall on the mountain, the electrical power went out in the neighborhood. All lights and sound crashed during the service and the sanctuary became very dark and cold. This was the first night of the meetings and I was getting ready to minister. Suddenly, I realized how much I depend on lights, sound, and heat instead of relying only on the Holy Spirit. It was a struggle for me to preach. I didn't adjust well to this unexpected, sudden change without electricity. And I was to be the guest minister there for three days!

The situation remained the same on the second day: no power. Oddly, I felt like I had no spiritual power in me, just as there was no electrical power at the meeting site. I was annoyed, anxious, and frustrated. I desperately tried praying to get victory over my struggle, but I couldn't break through. I decided to take a nap, which made me feel even worse. That night, I intended to preach on the topic of the Holy Spirit, but I felt totally unworthy to talk about Him because my emotions were such a mess. It was as though a dark cloud had descended over me during the previous service. Not only did I feel totally disqualified from talking about the Holy Spirit; I didn't even feel like preaching at all.

During worship, with only one microphone connected to a speaker powered by a generator, this revelation hit me: "You don't need electricity, lights, a microphone, or even heat to have the Holy Spirit show up. All you need is the cross. Jesus must be glorified. All you are glorifying right now are your emotions, prayer, and your nap!" I immediately redirected my attention from the problems to glorifying the power of Jesus. I took the focus off myself and turned my attention to Jesus, reminding myself that all the angels and inhabitants of heaven sing, "Worthy is the Lamb" (Revelation 5:11-12).

Everything shifted in my soul and faith rose up! A river of living water started to flow out of my spirit. It wasn't an emotion; it was a river. It wasn't something I tried to work up. Right before I got up to speak, the electricity came back on. But it did not matter anymore, because now, my dependence on the Holy Spirit within me was greater than the lights in the building. The Lord moved powerfully in that service. This is the lesson that marked my life that night: look to the cross if you want to experience the outpouring of the Holy Spirit. Truly, the Holy Spirit doesn't descend on our worthiness but on people who acknowledge the worthiness of Jesus and glorify Him and Him alone.

My dear friend, the Spirit manifests Himself whenever Jesus is glorified. If you want to draw on the fullness of the Holy Spirit, glorify Christ. Let what He did at Calvary be the uttermost thing in your mind and soul. If you value the cross, Pentecost will follow. If you want to have a Spirit-filled life, build your life on the sure foundation of Jesus' death, burial, and resurrection. Fire falls on the altar. The fire of the Holy Spirit falls on the sacrifice of Jesus, the Lamb of God. You are simply an altar, but Jesus is the sacrifice that attracts the fire of the Holy Spirit.

Rivers, not a Jacuzzi

In John 7, Christ compared a Spirit-filled life to rivers of living water (John 7:38). "Rivers" is plural, not singular. Let's compare it with John 4. While talking to the Samaritan woman, Jesus compared salvation to living water (John 4:10-14). There is a difference between living water and rivers of living water. At salvation, we receive the living water, but when we are walking in the Holy Spirit, we have access to abundant rivers of living water. The Holy Spirit is water from heaven.

Out of his heart will flow rivers of living water.
(John 7:38)

I love water, especially pools and jacuzzis. One of my favorite recreational activities is to sit in a hot tub. My dad had a nice hot tub and whenever it would snow, I would go with the guys to sit in the hot tub for a while, then roll in the snow and get back into the hot tub. It was so much fun and so relaxing! In fact, one of the reasons I have a gym membership is because my gym has a sauna, steam room, and hot tub. After a good workout I can reward myself with those relaxing pleasures. But as much as I like the hot tub, it is not a river. It has bubbles, but no life. The hot water is relaxing, but it cannot sustain life. It's hot, but it also contains a lot of chemicals.

I wonder how many times we have replaced the rivers of the Holy Spirit with the jacuzzi of the flesh. The mark of these last days, according to the apostle Paul, will be *"having a form of godliness but denying its power"* (2 Timothy 3:5). We have to guard our hearts, so we won't settle for a religious form or semblance without substance. Not having power of the Holy Spirit means not having an abundant life. That's what a hot tub is: it's a man-made, man-controlled thing, and it sure is relaxing and entertaining. Religion creates spiritual hot tubs, but Jesus gives us rivers of living water. The water He gives us quenches our thirst. Did you know you should not sit in a jacuzzi longer than 15 minutes because it dehydrates you? The rivers that Jesus offers not only hydrate you but flow out to quench the thirst of others as well, because rivers promote life.

A jacuzzi needs electricity to operate. Rivers generate electricity for that jacuzzi. One depends on outside power; the other provides the power. Without the river of God flowing through us, we are reduced to monuments instead of movements. When Lot's wife looked back, she became a pillar of salt. You and I are called to be people of salt here on earth, not pillars of salt. Pillars don't move, they are stationary, stuck in one place. People are meant to move. When believers are filled with the Holy Spirit, they become a movement. It's time to get loosened up spiritually. It's time to receive and release the river of the Holy Spirit and not settle for stationary ponds of religion. Look at your life now. Are you stuck in a routine life, not moving forward, tired of the same old things? Perhaps you've substituted the life-giving rivers for a man-made hot tub.

The words of Jesus on the last day of the feast are fitting and true for you today as well:

If anyone thirsts, let him come to Me and drink.

(John 7:37)

Come to the Living Water and have a drink. That drink will become a river. That river will keep you hydrated spiritually because it will never run dry. There is enough flowing water to keep you on course as you walk with God for the rest of your life. There is enough power in that river to help you conquer your flesh, devils, and the world. There is so much potential in that river that it will spontaneously flow out of you and impact those around you.

A Temple, not a Tomb

The prophet Ezekiel saw a vision of this living water flowing out of the temple (Ezekiel 47:1-12). The water speaks of the Holy Spirit flowing out of the believer, who is His temple. God made you His temple, not a tomb. Tombs are resting places for the dead. There are decorative stones, colorful flowers, and many good memories represented at a tomb, but life is not present. Jesus called religious people "tombs"—places where life used to be. They decorated their outward religious life with self-discipline but were utterly dead on the inside. Sin also turns the hearts of people into tombs of decay and death. But by the grace of God, through faith, Jesus takes a tomb and transforms it into a temple. We go from the grave to the garden. We go from hiding sin to hosting the Spirit—from living in secret sin to being a secret place for Him.

The Holy Spirit is holy. He can visit anyone, but He abides only in a holy place. Just as you and I don't eat from dirty plates or drink from dirty cups, the Holy Spirit does not inhabit unclean places. Jesus' finished work on the cross created an extreme makeover, turning a heart that was like a garbage dump into a dwelling place for the Holy Spirit. At salvation, God gave us a new nature, spirit, and identity so we could become prime real estate where the Holy Spirit would live. Jesus' death on the cross not only provided an eternal place in heaven for us, but also made us a habitation for the Holy Spirit to dwell in here on earth.

Temples don't erect themselves; someone else builds them. We were transformed into a temple by the work that Jesus Christ accomplished on the cross. Our good works can't turn us into an abiding place for the Holy Spirit. We don't become a dwelling of the Holy Spirit by our religious efforts. It's not about our works or efforts; it's by Jesus' death on the cross. The river will flow out of the temple—which is you—made to be a dwelling place for the Holy Spirit by the finished work of Jesus Christ.

The Dove Descends on the Lamb

All four Gospels record an account of the Holy Spirit descending as a dove upon Jesus at His baptism. Doves represent purity, innocence, and gentleness. A dove is a beautiful picture of the Holy Spirit.

Leonard Ravenhill[3] once said,

> "There are nine main feathers on the left and right wings of the dove. There are also nine gifts of the Holy

---

3   Leonard Ravenhill was one of Britain's foremost outdoor evangelists of the 20th century and an author who focused on prayer and revival.

Spirit and nine fruits of the Spirit. There are also five main tail feathers on a dove, which can represent the fivefold ministry gifts of apostles, prophets, evangelists, pastors, and teachers. The tail feathers of a dove are like the rudder of a ship—they assist in balance and direction in flight, just as the fivefold ministry gifts in the church bring balance to the body of Christ."

Wow! What a beautiful portrait of the precious Holy Spirit and His work.

When Jesus was baptized in the river, the Holy Spirit in the form of a dove descended upon Him, whom John the Baptist declared to be the Lamb of God. That day the Dove descended on the Lamb. Therefore:

- Without the Lamb, there would be no Dove.
- Without the sacrifice, there would be no fire.
- Without the cross, there would be no Pentecost.
- Without Jesus being glorified, there would be no release of the Holy Spirit.

The Dove in the Ark

The first time a dove is mentioned in the Bible was after the flood when Noah released one from the ark. This dove left the ark three separate times.

The first time, the dove returned to the ark because it found no resting place. This speaks of the Old Testament times when the Holy Spirit would only come upon certain people who were given special assignments, but He didn't reside in them.

The second time the dove left the ark, it came back with an olive leaf. This speaks of the gospel being declared by our Lord under the anointing of the Holy Spirit.

The third time the dove left the ark, it did not return. This speaks of the outpouring of the Holy Spirit upon the church as prophesied by the prophet Joel (Joel 2:28-29) and fulfilled on the day of Pentecost.

Let's take a closer look at this dove that was living in the ark. The ark saved Noah from the flood of God's judgment on the land and all its inhabitants. We can conclude that the ark was symbolic of the finished work of Jesus. It was made of wood just as the cross was. It had one door, which speaks of Jesus being the one and only door to salvation. There was only one window, which represents the Word of God. Inside was only one family, which represents the church. The dove resided in the ark, just as the Holy Spirit lives in those who trust in Jesus for their salvation.

Jesus' finished work on the cross is the ark that protects us from the judgment of God. Just as the dove lived in the ark, so the precious Holy Spirit dwells in those who are made righteous by faith and not by works. As the dove entered the ark through the window, so it is with the Holy Spirit whenever we open God's Word. It is the window through which we ought to view life, and the window through which the light of God's revelation comes to us. God's Spirit, who is the Author of God's Word, will flow freely into us and through our lives.

I can't emphasize this enough: the Holy Spirit dwells in our temple. To experience the release of the Holy Spirit, we must daily cultivate an ongoing relationship with Jesus. This is our most important relationship on earth!

Baptism *of* and *in* the Holy Spirit

The writer of Hebrews told us that the doctrine of baptisms is one of the fundamental doctrines of Christian belief (Hebrews 6:1-2). You have probably heard of at least two baptisms: water baptism and baptism in the Holy Spirit. But the New Testament speaks of more than two baptisms. It actually shows us seven baptisms: the baptism of the Holy Spirit, the baptism in the Holy Spirit and fire, the baptism of suffering, the baptism into the cloud, the baptism into Moses, the baptism of John, and water baptism. That's a lot of baptisms!

The Greek word for baptism is *baptizo[4],* which means immersion. It signifies being fully submerged; it's not a sprinkling or pouring water on a person. When Jesus was baptized in the Jordan River, the Bible says He came "up from the water" (Matt. 3:16). Therefore, He was fully immersed into that water. Let me explain the difference between the baptism *of* the Holy Spirit and the baptism *in* the Holy Spirit. The baptism *of* the Holy Spirit is being fully immersed into the body of Christ, which is His church; the baptism *in* the Holy Spirit is about being fully immersed into the Spirit.

Remember how when you got baptized, whether in the baptistry or in the river, you went completely into the water? That's what the baptism *of* the Holy Spirit is: He immerses you fully into the Lord Jesus Christ and His church, which happens at the moment of salvation. Following that, Jesus baptizes you *into* the Holy Spirit, meaning He immerses you fully into His Spirit.

The baptism *of* or *by* the Holy Spirit is done by the Holy Spirit; the baptism *in* or *into* the Holy Spirit is done by Jesus. John the Baptist declared that Jesus would baptize people with fire and with the Holy

---

4 "G907 - baptizō - Strong's Greek Lexicon (kjv)." Blue Letter Bible. Web. 29 Mar, 2023. https://www.blueletterbible.org/lexicon/g907/kjv/tr/0-1/

Spirit. When you get saved, you experience the baptism *of* the Holy Spirit. When you get filled with the Holy Spirit, it is Jesus who does that. On the day of the Pentecost feast, it was Jesus who was baptizing believers *into* the Holy Spirit. The Spirit baptizes you, making you a member of His body, but Jesus baptizes you *into* His Spirit to equip you for service in His kingdom.

The baptism *of* (or by) the Holy Spirit makes you a member of the church or the body of Jesus; the baptism *in* the Holy Spirit is immersion into the realm of His power and spiritual authority. The Holy Spirit implants us into the Person of Christ.

> *For by one Spirit we were all baptized into one body—*
> *whether Jews or Greeks, whether slaves or free—and*
> *have all been made to drink into one Spirit.*
>
> **(1 Corinthians 12:13)**

That's why at our salvation, Scripture declares that we are in Christ. In Christ, we are a new creation. There is no condemnation to those who are in Christ. And do you know how we got to be in Christ? It was the work of the Holy Spirit. We were baptized into Christ by the Holy Spirit. God looks at us and sees Jesus because we are in Him.

The baptism *of* or *by* the Holy Spirit precedes baptism *in* the Holy Spirit. Every Christian was baptized *by* the Holy Spirit at the time of their salvation. The baptism *of* the Holy Spirit happens when we receive Jesus and His salvation; at that time, the Holy Spirit does the miracle of implanting us into Jesus. In fact, we can't be a part of the body of Jesus and His church without the baptizing work *of* the Holy Spirit. The baptism *of* the Holy Spirit is not about tongues or power but is about being immersed into Jesus—into His body, which is His church. Then, following that initial baptism, Jesus immerses us into the Holy Spirit, who then enables us to serve God with power. The baptism *in* the Holy Spirit is done by Jesus the Baptizer.

In the next chapter, we will look at one of the most misunderstood topics for many Christians: the conviction of the Holy Spirit. In order to develop a relationship with the Holy Spirit, you must understand the truth about the conviction of the Holy Spirit.

Three Convictions

The Conviction of the Holy Spirit

Chapter 2

*And when He has come, He will convict the world of sin,
and of righteousness, and of judgment: of sin, because
they do not believe in Me.*

(John 16:8-9)

*J*esus said that when the Holy Spirit comes, He will convict the world of sin and bring conviction of their unbelief. People of the world don't naturally believe in Jesus as their Savior and Lord. Therefore, the Holy Spirit's main assignment here on the earth is to point people to the cross so they may believe in Jesus for their salvation. He doesn't draw attention to Himself but directs all attention to Jesus.

Reading a lot about the Holy Spirit and listening to sermons about Him should increase your love and passion for Jesus. If not, something is wrong! I fear that most teaching exalts the Holy Spirit and not Jesus Christ, the almighty Son of God. There was a point in Jesus's lifetime when the people tried to make Him their king, but He simply walked away. Wasn't Jesus a King? You bet He was and still is! Is He the Ruler of the earth? Of course He is! But the reason He came to earth two thousand years ago wasn't to reign, but to serve, to love, and to die. He rode on a donkey, not a horse. He came as a lamb, not as a lion. Yes, He is indeed returning to earth as King, but His first advent was as the Suffering Servant.

And so it is with the Holy Spirit—He is God, powerful and majestic. He is here on earth right now among believers, but He has no desire to be exalted, praised, or glorified! His main assignment within the Trinity is to put all the focus on Jesus, especially His finished work of salvation on the cross. The Spirit's job is to promote the glory of Jesus Christ. This is His one and only purpose on earth today; it is not to glorify Himself. Jesus said, *"When He, the Spirit of truth, has come... He will glorify Me"* (John 16:13-14). But so often, we are in danger of making the Holy Spirit what we think He should be and exalting Him, just as people did when they tried to make Jesus their earthly king. If we don't allow the Holy Spirit to glorify Christ alone, and direct our full attention toward Him, our relationship with the Holy Spirit will not mature.

Conviction of the Holy Spirit: Unbelief

The Holy Spirit's first and foremost conviction is to the world, not to believers. He convicts the world of one predominant sin. That sin is not just fornicating, stealing, murder, homosexuality, smoking, or drinking, although these are vile acts of disobedience to our holy God. Those who practice these things don't live in harmony with God in His kingdom. But the sin the Holy Spirit mainly wants to convict the world of is the sin of unbelief, or the fact that they don't personally believe in Jesus as the one and only way to God and salvation (John 14:6).

As I grew up in church, I often heard references about the conviction of the Holy Spirit. It was always connected with the Holy Spirit convicting a believer of some sin. While it's true that the Holy Spirit points out sin in a believer's life, His primary assignment is to convict the world of their unbelief. Without faith in Jesus's substitutionary death on the cross, no one can enjoy eternal life with Him. As important as it is to be pure, faithful in marriage, not cheat on your taxes, not smoke and drink, not steal and lie, these moral virtues in and of themselves don't bring us into an eternal relationship with God. These moral acts can keep us out of jail, but not out of hell. Merely trying to avoid sinning will not save your soul. You must turn to God so that your sins may be blotted out (Acts 3:19). There is only one way to the heavenly Father, and that is by believing in His Son, Jesus, for the forgiveness of your sins (John 14:6). There is only one road to heaven, and that is by the way of the cross of Calvary. The Holy Spirit is like the navigation system in a car, advising the driver to take an immediate turn toward Christ to reach the destination of being reconciled to the Creator.

I remember when a young man once approached me in the lobby of our church and asked me if it's okay for him to smoke pot. This young man wasn't a follower of Christ, but I knew that he and his family attended our church. I replied to him, "For you, it's not wrong to smoke pot since it's legal in our state." He looked at me puzzled, and continued, "What about drinking?" I said, "Go ahead and drink as well; it's legal, and you should drink as much as you can—just don't drink and drive." He was shocked! Others overheard the conversation and started to gather around to hear the pastor giving people a license to smoke and drink. I continued, "John (not his real name), you are going to hell. Both you and I know that, and your family knows it too. You are not a believer in the Savior, Jesus Christ, and you don't want to repent. So, what difference will it make if you go to hell as a pothead or a nonsmoker? Do you think that if you quit smoking, you will go to heaven? No, we don't go to heaven just because we don't smoke or drink. So, if I were you, I would smoke and drink and do all the bad things my flesh desires, since I'm already going to hell at least I didn't hold myself back from what my flesh desired." He looked at me like a deer blinded in headlights. I didn't say anything shocking; I just gave him the gospel from a different angle than he was used to hearing it. That night, he gave his life to Jesus.

Please hear me, we are not saved by doing good works; we are saved to do good works. We are only saved by having personal faith in Jesus's finished work of salvation on the cross. This faith, when genuine, naturally produces good works (James 2:17). This dreadful sin of unbelief simply means that folks don't personally trust in Jesus who shed His blood on the cross. He paid the ransom for their redemption from condemnation.

> *He who believes in Him is not condemned; but he*
> *who does not believe is condemned already, because*
> *he has not believed in the name of the only begotten*
> *Son of God.*
>
> **(John 3:18)**

The gospel is not just about behavior modification, but heart transformation. Attempting to please God with good works without repentance toward God and faith in Christ Jesus is like putting perfume on a corpse. It will smell good, but it's still dead. In the same way, dressing up a dead man in a nice suit will not make him breathe again. Yeah, he will look good, but he is dead. DEAD! Religion tries to make bad people good; the Holy Spirit makes dead people alive. That's why He convicts the world of the first and foremost sin: unbelief. Through believing the gospel, the spiritually dead person becomes alive by the work of the same Holy Spirit and is empowered to do good works.

Once the Holy Spirit convicts us of our sin of unbelief, we want to repent of how we viewed the Lord Jesus Christ, and then we place our total trust in Him. This same Holy Spirit, who was initially with us to lead us to Jesus, now comes to live in us to make us more like Jesus. Did you catch that? The Spirit, who was with us before salvation, comes to live in us at the moment of salvation. Consequently, the Holy Spirit begins the work of growing us in the Lord. Yes, the Holy Spirit is with everyone who is not a Christian; He is with them to convict them of their sin of unbelief in Jesus. That's why unbelievers can testify that they felt the nearness of God at times. This is totally normal because here on this earth, the Holy Spirit is with every person to convict them of their unbelief. Once they believe the gospel, He is no longer just with them; He is invited to live in them. Jesus said to His disciples:

> *The Spirit of truth, whom the world cannot receive,*
> *because it neither sees Him nor knows Him; but you*
> *know Him, for He dwells with you and will be in you.*
>
> **(John 14:17)**

The disciples knew about the Holy Spirit. He was around them the entire three years they followed Jesus. They saw countless miracles, healings, and demonic deliverances, but Jesus spoke of a time when this same Holy Spirit would come to live in them. That happened after Jesus's resurrection. Let me sum this up:

- *"And when He had said this, He breathed on them, and said to them, 'Receive the Holy Spirit.'"* (John 20:22)

- The Holy Spirit came to be with them, and a few weeks later, on the day of Pentecost, the Holy Spirit came upon them for ministry.

- The Holy Spirit is with us before salvation to convict us of sin.

- The Holy Spirit is in us at salvation to produce godly character.

- The Holy Spirit is upon us for service.

Conviction vs. Condemnation

So, the Holy Spirit convicts the world of sin in order that they may believe in Jesus. Once they put their trust in Jesus, the same Holy Spirit who was with them initially, comes to live inside of them. He continues to convict the born-again believers, but His conviction is totally different now. Instead of convicting new believers of sin, He convicts them of righteousness, not condemnation.

This was such a shock to me. My idea of the Holy Spirit's conviction was that if I felt bad about myself, it was the Holy Spirit who was convicting me. Condemnation and conviction felt the same for me, and I had a hard time telling the difference. Like water and alcohol, they look the same, but they have such different results.

Conviction is specific; condemnation is general. Conviction says, "You spoke harshly to your wife." Condemnation says, "You are a worthless husband." The Holy Spirit will highlight a specific behavior that needs to be changed; the devil will throw you under the bus. Conviction attacks the issue; condemnation attacks your identity.

Conviction is from the Holy Spirit; condemnation is from the devil, the accuser of the brethren (Revelation 12:10).

The devil will use your occasional sin to tell you that you are a sinner, but you have to reject that dirty lie. *"There is therefore now no condemnation to those who are in Christ Jesus"* (Romans 8:1). You are in Christ, and therefore, condemnation is not your portion. The Spirit of Jesus might shine a light on some area in your life that needs to be repented of, but the devil will try to put you back into the mindset of a sinner. No, you are not a sinner; you are a child of God! You are born again! Your issue is not the loss of your identity, because your real identity is Jesus Christ!

Conviction gives you hope; condemnation makes you hopeless. When the Holy Spirit convicts, the light comes on. Hope is released. Change is imminent. Godly sorrow and repentance follow. But condemnation is the very opposite; you feel like you are a total loser, a failure, and you can't change.

> *For godly sorrow produces repentance leading to salvation, not to be regretted; but the sorrow of the world produces death.*
>
> **(2 Corinthians 7:10)**

Conviction leads to repentance; condemnation leads to remorse. Repentance makes you better; remorse makes things worse.

Remorse only produces guilt, shame, and regret.

Conviction of the Holy Spirit: Righteousness

When was the last time you were convicted of righteousness? Did you know that this is the Holy Spirit's primary conviction for believers? Righteousness is more than having our sins forgiven. Righteousness is more than going to heaven. It's right standing with God that empowers right living before men.

You are righteous through Christ, but I'm pretty sure you don't feel righteous all the time. That's why the Holy Spirit seeks to convict you of this truth. The Holy Spirit wants to move us out of religious rags to the righteousness of Christ. But beware! This righteousness is not a result of you doing righteous deeds. Jesus said:

Of righteousness, because I go to My Father and you see Me no more.

(John 16:10)

The righteousness that the Holy Spirit convicts us of is related to Jesus, not to our good works and virtues. Jesus not only took upon himself our sin on the cross, but it says in 2 Corinthians 5:21:

For He made Him who knew no sin to be sin for us, that we might become the righteousness of God in Him.

Paul tells us that Jesus became sin on the cross. That's more than taking our sin—He became sin for us so we can be righteous.

When Jesus was talking with Nicodemus, He told him something strange. Before the well-known verse in John 3:16, *"For God so loved the world,"* Jesus said, *"And as Moses lifted up the serpent in the wilderness, even so must the Son of Man be lifted up."* (John 3:14)

Did you notice that Jesus compared Himself to a serpent? We all know that Jesus is the Lamb of God who takes away the sin of the world, but being lifted up as a serpent seems to be a bit off. The serpent is the devil, and snakes are viewed as evil. Out of so many shadows and types in the Old Testament that Jesus could have used to reveal His mission on earth, He chose the one with the snake on the pole. It doesn't seem consistent with His nature to be compared to a snake.

Let me recall this story to you: when the nation of Israel was complaining in the wilderness, God sent poisonous snakes to bite them. And when they, in panic, cried out for help, the Lord did not hurry to heal them. Instead, He instructed Moses to craft a bronze serpent and lift it high on a pole so that whoever looked at it would be cured (Numbers 21:8-9). All they had to do was look up at the snake. Likewise, Jesus was lifted up on the cross so that whoever looks to Him with a believing heart will live and be cured of the serpent's deadly venom.

As a lamb, Jesus paid for my sin; but as a serpent, He became my sin (2 Corinthians 5:21). Jesus was made to be sin on the cross, which is much more than just paying for my sin. He became sin. In the same way a rod was created to be a bronze snake, Christ was made to be sin on the cross. Moses didn't lift up a live snake; it was a man-made snake. So it is with Christ: He was not a sinner; He was made to be sin on the cross. He didn't become sin by sinning, but by submitting to His Father's will. Jesus obeyed so that you and I could become righteous, not by our own works of righteousness, but by receiving right standing in God's eyes—the gift of righteousness.

Jesus became sin by the act of surrender, so that you will instantly become righteous by faith. God did not consider the fact that His Son Jesus had been sinless in body, soul, and spirit before hanging on the cross. The Father turned His back on Him because Jesus was actually sin while dying there on the cross! In the same way, God considers you to be the righteousness of Christ, even if your character is still going through changes. It takes time to become Christlike in your thinking, your talk, and your actions. God accepts you when you have Christ in your heart because you are declared righteous, even if you haven't done even one righteous deed yet.

I became righteous the same way that Jesus became sin! That's called grace, which I accepted through trust and surrender! It's more than the mere forgiveness of all my sins; it's a change of status in the eyes of God. If Jesus died as a sinner, even though He wasn't one, then I can live as a righteous person even if I don't feel like one. That's what the Holy Spirit had to convict me of, something I couldn't reconcile in my mind. I had seen the Holy Spirit as a faultfinder, always pointing out my mistakes. But Jesus revealed to me that the Holy Spirit's job is not only to disclose what needs improvement, but to shed light on what's right with me. I don't mean that He will emphasize what good works I have done; He will convict me of Jesus's righteousness which now abides in me, and not my own self-righteousness. That's so awesome!

All I need to do is heed this conviction of the Holy Spirit and follow His instructions. Just as Moses told the entire nation to look to the bronze snake on the pole, the Holy Spirit tells us today to look to the cross of Calvary—not at our personal feelings of guilt and shame.

Don't get obsessed with snake bites; look to the One who became a serpent on our behalf.

Israel needed the redemption lamb in Egypt, but in the wilderness, they needed a bronze serpent. The lamb brought salvation; the bronze serpent brought sanctification. The lamb broke sin's bondage; the serpent healed snake bites.

The cross of Jesus is not only for our salvation but also for our sanctification. If we glance at it, we find salvation; but if we gaze at it, we find transformation. If you have received Jesus as a lamb, continue to gaze upon Him as a bronze serpent. We must get a revelation of our righteousness. We need to accept the Holy Spirit's conviction of our righteousness in Christ.

When the devil tells you that you are not righteous, remind him that Jesus died a sinner's death so you can live a righteous life, even though He Himself wasn't a sinner! When the chatter of your past memories and guilt tells you that you are not righteous because you fell, remind yourself that Jesus was considered sin even though He didn't sin. Remind the memories of your past that your righteousness is from God, not from right works. Replace those haunting memories with the truth. When your feelings come against you, saying that you're not good enough, remind them of the fact that you are going to reign victoriously in life by God's grace and His gift of righteousness. You can live righteously because Jesus was crucified and became sin on your behalf.

Conviction of the Holy Spirit: Judgment

Of judgment, because the ruler of this world is judged.
(John 16:11)

The Holy Spirit comes to convict people of these three things: sin, righteousness, and judgment. Sin came through Adam. Righteousness came through Christ. Judgment came to Satan. The Holy Spirit is not here to convict Satan of his coming judgment, because the devil is unable to change his ways. He was never offered a chance to repent and be saved. The Spirit convicts us of our enemy's judgment and defeat because Jesus brought a death blow to the devil's kingdom when He arose from the grave.

The devil bragged to Jesus about his authority over all the kingdoms of the world, but after the cross, Jesus boldly proclaimed that all authority is His. The cross of Jesus pronounced judgment on the devil for his treason against God's kingdom.

Now is the judgment of this world; now the ruler of this world will be cast out.
(John 12:31)

The devil is currently in exile while here on this earth. Every time we preach the gospel of Jesus Christ, we pronounce judgment on the kingdom of darkness. Every time we cast out demons, we deal another blow of defeat to the enemy.

Just as David went up against Goliath and took him out of circulation, our Savior, who is David's son, dealt a death blow to the enemy on the cross. The Israeli soldiers who faced Goliath were a bunch of cowards, but when David slew the giant, they were instantly energized by that victory and advanced against the enemy's troops. That's what Christ did for us. He invigorated the pronounced judgment on the giant by taking him down. Jesus's victory is our portion. His triumph empowers us to fight. The Holy Spirit is using the victory that Jesus accomplished to empower us soldiers to victoriously fight the defeated foe.

And when the Philistines saw that their champion was dead, they fled. Now the men of Israel and Judah arose and shouted, and pursued the Philistines.

(1 Samuel 17:51b-52a)

Satan has already been judged. Oh yes, he will also be judged in the future and cast into the lake of fire. That's his future! But right now, we are on the battlefield with Jesus, the son of David. When King Jesus made a move against the leader of the opposing kingdom, He defeated their champion. The enemy is on the run to this very day. That's why the Bible says to resist him and he will flee (James 4:7). We aren't called to run from the devil; he is going to run from us! The only thing we run from is sin—not from Satan. That's why we minister deliverance and cast out demons. Christians are like spiritual police; the devil is a thug, a criminal, and a fugitive on the run.

Just as the soldiers of Israel arose and shouted and pursued, today we also rise up and shout victory by faith with the Holy Spirit's conviction that our foe is defeated. We rise up and fight. We rise up and drive out devils. We rise up and pronounce judgment on the devil. We rise up and pursue freedom for others. We don't fight for victory; we fight from victory. It's time to wreak havoc on the kingdom of darkness. It's time to share in the glorious spoils of Jesus's victory on the cross.

In the next chapter, we will look closely at the type of gifts that our triune God offers to every believer. Before we can open the gift of the Holy Spirit, we must receive the gift of the Father and the Son.

The Gifts of the Trinity

The Communion of the Holy Spirit

Chapter 3

*The grace of the Lord Jesus Christ, and the love of
God, and the communion of the Holy Spirit be with
you all. Amen.*

(2 Corinthians 13:14)

The verse above is the first verse I memorized as a child growing up in the church because the congregation I attended
recited it at the dismissal of every service (2 Corinthians
13:14). Only later in my walk with the Lord did the depth of this verse
become more real. If you really want to know the Holy Spirit as a
Person, this one verse holds a gold mine of revelation.

Paul, in his second letter to the church in Corinth, brings the
three Persons of the Trinity into a picture of unity, showing us how
each Person of the Trinity has something to offer to a believer: Jesus
brings grace, the Father offers love, and the Spirit gives communion.

The Gift of Jesus

The grace of the Lord Jesus Christ, and the love of God, and the communion of the Holy Spirit be with you all. Amen.

(2 Corinthians 13:14)

Jesus offers us the gift of grace, which is His unmerited favor. Through this grace, we are saved. Grace is different from mercy. Mercy takes away what we do deserve; grace gives us what we don't deserve. Last year around Christmas time, I was driving to church for the morning prayer time and didn't notice that my speed was fifteen miles per hour over the speed limit. While on my way, I stopped at a drive-through to get some coffee. While waiting for my coffee, I told the barista about our church and invited her to come. After getting my coffee, I got back on the road and heard a siren. I got pulled over and received a ticket. It turns out that the police officer had been following me and was waiting to give me a ticket. He was kind enough to let me finish my order and get my coffee first. I got what I deserved. That's justice.

The police officer kindly reduced my citation to only ten miles over the limit instead of fifteen. What I got was justice. I deserved that ticket. Mercy would have been if I had never gotten the ticket. Grace, on the other hand, would have been if that police officer had paid for my coffee instead of giving me a ticket. I know you're thinking that would be crazy and probably against the law to let a speeding driver go free. Who would do that? Jesus did! That's why it's called amazing grace; it's more than mercy. Jesus offers grace to us.

Surely goodness and mercy shall follow me all the days
of my life.

(Psalm 23:6)

I had an officer follow me to give me justice, but every believer has God's goodness, grace, and mercy following them. You're being followed! But before you receive the gift of the Holy Spirit, you have to unwrap the gift of grace. The revelation of the grace of God is the foundation for the communion of the Holy Spirit.

At the house where we used to live, someone broke in and ransacked all my stuff, but took nothing except a car that was in the garage. By the way, the car wasn't mine. It had been loaned to me by my cousin who was planning to give it to someone in need. A few hours later after stealing the car, the thief left it downtown with a note, "I am sorry for taking your car." The police got involved. I had a blurry picture of that person, so I made a Facebook post to try to find him. No, I wasn't trying to find him so I could press charges and bring him to justice. Instead, my cousin and I had ultimately decided to give the car to the very man who had stolen it, with the hope that it would bring him to Christ. Mercy would be to refuse to press charges, but grace is above mercy—it gives what the other person doesn't deserve. The only reason my cousin and I would even consider this act of kindness is because that's exactly what Jesus did for us. Unfortunately, we never found that needy person to whom we wanted to extend grace.

And that's the person whom Jesus is searching for today as well. You and I were criminals—sinful offenders. We offended God and broke His law. But He resolved that issue of transgression on the cross; and today, He is looking for us to turn ourselves in so He can forgive us, restore us, and show us His grace. Sadly, most of us don't really believe that Jesus is so good that He would want to bless us with kindness and favor. We feel undeserving of His grace. We feel like we've made way too many mistakes that disqualify us from His love. When I was looking for that guy who broke into my house, I wasn't waiting for him to become worthy or deserving. I wanted to give him what he didn't deserve. All he needed to do was trust that I wouldn't turn on him. Grace is received by faith. It takes faith to trust that God is so very good when we are not good at all.

There is a beautiful Old Testament picture of Jesus's grace in the life of king David. David was trying to show goodness to Jonathan's son, Mephibosheth, who'd fallen at a young age and was crippled in his feet. Mephibosheth wasn't worthy. His dad had died in battle. His grandpa had mental issues and was rejected by God. Besides that, he wanted to kill David. But David wanted to be kind to his friend's son. The covenant that David had previously made with Jonathan was the source of that goodness. It took humility on the part of the crippled man to not wallow in his misery and self-pity, but to trust the king's kindness and respond accordingly. Receiving that grace changed his life. Instead of laboring hard in his fields, he was seated at the king's table daily. Even though his legs weren't cured, his crippled legs were covered by the table. That is a beautiful story of grace.

The story of Mephibosheth is recorded in 2 Samuel 9:1-13 and in the next chapter, David tried to do the same thing for someone else. He tried to show kindness to neighboring king Hanun because of the amiable relationship David had with his father, the late king Nahash. The response was entirely different. Instead of trusting David's kindness, Hanun became suspicious. He doubted David's motives. It started a conflict that resulted in a war, which eventually led to Hanun's defeat and the demise of the people he ruled. Look at the differences in these two stories:

- Both men had the offer of goodness extended.

- Both men responded differently.

- Both men ended up in different places.

The gift of grace can either be received or rejected. It takes faith to accept it, and fear will push you to reject it. Jesus is that good. He offers grace. He desires to shower you with His unmerited favor.

The Gift of the Father

*The grace of the Lord Jesus Christ, and **the love of God,** and the communion of the Holy Spirit be with you all. Amen.*

(2 Corinthians 13:14)

Every family has their own Christmas traditions, and ours include meeting with the family on Christmas morning and giving gifts to each other. We usually go through a website and pick someone in the family to whom we will give a gift, but the parents give gifts to each of their children. All three members of the Trinity give something to the believer: Jesus gives grace, the Father offers love, and the Spirit gives communion.

Let's unwrap the gift of the Father. Love is the deepest emotional need of every human being. It's also the biggest deficit in our generation. We are not just physical beings that need sleep and food; we have a need in our souls to be loved and to feel truly accepted. Many don't feel loved or wanted, and so many others don't feel lovable. Our generation is starving for love. The devil offers lust to try to quench that hunger, but love and lust aren't the same. As I said, water and alcohol may look the same, but they have different effects on those who are drinking them. The same is true with love and lust—the absence of knowing God's love creates a vacuum where lust thrives.

In our generation, fatherless households contribute to lust in young people. *If anyone loves the world, the love of the Father is not in him* (1 John 2:15). Love for the world only grows when a father's love is absent. So many have grown up with fathers completely absent from their lives. When these kids become adults, they raise their families the same way they were raised. And unfortunately, there are also many of us who grew up with fathers being there physically, but who didn't show us love and affection.

In my early years, I struggled with feelings of not being loved by my father. However, I had the best parents in the world. They have been married for over 35 years now and set an example of what it means to follow God and to provide for their family. My dad, who is probably the smartest man I know, did not show his affections. It was just not a part of his culture to be affectionate and to verbally express affirmation. For a long time, I felt like I failed him by not being who he wanted me to be. My dad is a handyman, and he is good at fixing a car or building a house. He even built his own sauna and steam room. That's who my dad is. On the other hand, I am good at breaking things. I went into full-time ministry at the age of 16 and never had a job outside of the church. For a long time, I had the feeling that my dad wished I would be someone else or do something else. He never voiced it, but I felt it. He never expressed his approval or affirmation of me serving God, nor did he say he was proud of me doing what I was doing for God's kingdom.

I know you might be thinking that I am being a crybaby and need to get over myself, but really, I'm only sharing how I felt. I had a very difficult time talking with him. I would get in a car and ride with him for an hour but have nothing to say or ask. I could easily and freely talk to strangers, but not to my dad. Honestly, it hurt me deeply. One time, when my father went to Lowe's to get some construction materials (Lowe's and Home Depot are his favorite stores), a check-out cashier looked at his last name. She asked if he knew Vladimir Savchuk. He said, "Yes, that's my son." So, my dad came home and started bragging about how the cashier noticed his last name. I knew that nobody knows our last name in town unless they know me, so I was hoping that my dad would finally say that he was proud of me.

It was probably silly of me to imagine that, but I thought this was my moment; my dad might say something nice about me in front of the family. But the only thing he continued talking about was how she recognized his last name and the discounts he got. That was the first time I recall that I went to my room and wept over my longing to be affirmed by my own dad. I got compliments from so many other people, but that's not what a son needs—he yearns for his father's affirmation. So, over the next few years I tried to prove to him that I was worthy of approval; and of course, I failed miserably.

When my dad was building a new house, I tried my best to go and help him as much as I could in my free time. The problem was that I am totally inept at construction. My best attempts to help him only made things worse. I remember like it was yesterday, the time I went to the construction site right after work to help cut some tile for him. I imagined that once I cut the tile and helped him with building the house, he would be proud of me. My dad had a supply of exotic tiles in a limited quantity for his project. I cut every piece wrong and broke some tiles by accident. Finally, Dad asked me to leave the construction site and go home so I wouldn't break any more things. I was embarrassed and felt stupid and worthless. The worst part was that my attempt to win his affirmation failed terribly. I attempted a few more things to get his approval, only to fail again and again. I got so tired of trying, but I was afraid to voice my frustrations to him. He never abused me or did bad things to me. I knew that my dad loved but I didn't feel it. I felt guilty for my mixed-up feelings, which only added another layer of confusion. I took this to the Lord in prayer many times. I would pour out my heart and ask God to change me or change my dad. Well, God changed me!

This change came from a very unusual place. I was already married, and a few years into our marriage, we went to a sushi restaurant. They brought us an appetizer. My view of appetizers is like the ones you get at the Olive Garden restaurant with unlimited salad, soup, and breadsticks. But this Japanese place brought us a big plate with only four or five leaves on it. I was like, "What? That's it? How am I supposed to be fed by this? This is ridiculous," I told my wife. She said something that the Holy Spirit reminded me of the next day in my prayer time to bring healing of an orphan heart. My wife replied, "An appetizer is not the main course; it's only meant to whet your appetite and prepare you for the main meal." After eating my few leaves, or what some might call a salad, I waited impatiently for the main course. And later I left that place feeling well fed.

The next morning in prayer, the Holy Spirit told me clearly and loudly, "Your dad is the appetizer, and I am your main meal." He said, "You are expecting too much of him and too little of Me." Some fathers are like Japanese appetizers with just a few leaves, and some are like an Olive Garden unlimited salad, but they are never meant to be the main meal. I wept like I had never wept before, and I felt the Father's love finally being poured into my heart by the Holy Spirit.

The light went on in my mind: my dad did the best he could! I would have to accept whatever love he gave me and get even more hungry for God's abounding love. An encounter with the boundless love of the Father healed my heart.

After that, I no longer went fishing for love and affirmation from my father; I moved on to honoring and serving him as a son. My construction skills changed and, seriously, I stopped breaking tiles. Whenever I would go to help him, I actually helped without breaking things. I was freed from doing things for him just to get affirmation; I was there to serve him. And, the night that changed my relationship with my father happened when I preached at an event in Sacramento, California. After the meeting, my dad texted me how proud he and my mom were of who I had become, how they couldn't ask for a better son than me, and how they both wept when I was preaching. I had been waiting to hear those words for a long time, but God wanted me to get healed first by His love before he would bring that affirmation from my dad.

Today, I have an amazing relationship with my dad. I am not only affirmed by my heavenly Father but also by my earthly dad. He watches all my streams, and when I travel, he is always there on live stream, chatting and commenting and sending SMS messages of love and support after each sermon. He and my mom became monthly partners of my ministry as well. God truly healed my heart and He changed theirs.

The gift of the Father's love is the main course that will satisfy your longing for acceptance. Maybe your parents aren't there for you, and you're desperately longing for their love and affirmation. Perhaps you got a skimpy appetizer in life; but God is your main course. Feast on His love, which He so freely provides for you. You didn't come *from* your parents; you came *through* your parents. You don't own your parents, and you can't expect them to do what you think they should do. God is your true Dad. Run into His arms and let Him embrace you. Let His love heal your wounds. Allow Him to affirm you.

"For God so loved the world that He gave His only begotten Son" (John 3:16). May I remind you that God didn't send Jesus out of pity for sinners. Not even out of compassion. Jesus didn't come because God felt sorry for you. He LOVED you. His motive was love. You and I had nothing to offer Him except our sin and weakness, but He still loved us. He "so loved the world." He so loved—not just liked—the world. He *so* loved, not *just* loved. Basic and normal love would have been enough but not for Him. He SO loved. He "so loved the world" speaks of loving unrighteous sinners, evildoers, and fallen people living in sin.

If He had that much love for us when we were a mess, can you imagine how much love He has for us now that we are His sons and daughters? Stop mentally punishing those who didn't love you in life, and start receiving the revelation that God really, really loves you! Stop stressing over feeling a lack of love for God and start thinking about the overflow of His love for you. Because God loves you so much, it's a good time to stop hating yourself. You can be healed in the flood of the Father's love. Insecurity dies in that love. Inferiority gets drowned in that love. The feeling of unworthiness disappears because love overcomes it. What people did to you or what they said about you, begins to lose its hold over you when this revelation grips you. This love turns wounds into scars and scars into stars. Can you pause and just ponder the amazing love He has for you? This is your next step toward the Holy Spirit. The fellowship of the Spirit follows the love of the Father. You can't enjoy divine fellowship if you don't embrace the gift of grace and love.

The Gift of the Holy Spirit

The grace of the Lord Jesus Christ, and the love of
*God, and **the communion of the Holy Spirit be with***
***you all**. Amen.*

(2 Corinthians 13:14)

Just as Jesus offers *grace* and the Father offers *love*, the Holy Spirit also has a gift for every child of God. That gift is not power, even though He fills us with power. That offer is not tongues, even though we will speak in unknown tongues after being filled with the Spirit. He offers us His communion or divine fellowship, which is the key to walking in the Holy Spirit. It's important to notice that it doesn't say communion *with* the Holy Spirit, but it refers to His communion that He desires to give us. Of course, we know that communion is a two-way street, but the emphasis is on the communion coming from the Holy Spirit. He is the one who initiates fellowship with us.

The Holy Spirit is the initiator. Notice that the passage says, *the grace of Jesus*, not grace *with* Jesus. Jesus has grace to extend to us. So it is with the love *of* the Father, not love *with* or *for* the Father. The Father is the giver of this love, and we respond by returning love back to Him after receiving that gift. Those are their gifts to us. They are what the three Persons of the Trinity offer to us, not what we can offer to them! The Holy Spirit extends the offer of His communion. The only reason we can have the communion with the Holy Spirit is because He yearns to have communion with us.

The Holy Spirit wants to have communion with you, which is not the same as conviction. "Communion" does not mean giving orders, nor does it mean leading or directing, or even teaching or empowering. Yes, the Spirit does all these things—He guides, directs, teaches, and convicts. But Paul reveals that the Holy Spirit wants to have fellowship with us just as much as Jesus wants to give us grace and the Father wants to shower us with love. "Communion" in Greek is *koinōnia*[5], which means participation in social relations, fellowship, distribution, association, community, or joint participation. This word is mentioned about 20 times in the New Testament. Let me share one example of it:

> *And they continued steadfastly in the apostles' doctrine*
> *and fellowship, in the breaking of bread, and in prayers.*
> **(Acts 2:42)**

The early church believers spent time in fellowship with each other. We all know what that looks like: talking, chatting, eating, having a good time, sharing, and enjoying one another's company.

Fellowship is not prayer; it's friendship. When you fellowship with your brothers and sisters, you're not praying to them; you're talking with them. That's what the Holy Spirit wants with us. Communion of the Holy Spirit is conversation with a believer. The Holy Spirit wants to have an ongoing conversation with you in your spirit, not just in your prayer time or while listening to a sermon or reading your Bible, but at all times.

The best example is Jesus and His disciples. Since the Holy Spirit was to be "another" Helper, Jesus declared:

---

5   "G2842 - koinōnia - Strong's Greek Lexicon (kjv)." Blue Letter Bible. Web. 29 Mar, 2023. https://www.blueletterbible.org/lexicon/g2842/kjv/tr/0-1/.

And I will pray the Father, and He will give you another
Helper, that He may abide with you forever—the Spirit
of truth, whom the world cannot receive, because it
neither sees Him nor knows Him; but you know Him, for
He dwells with you and will be in you. I will not leave
you orphans; I will come to you.

(John 14:16-18)

The title "Helper" is a translation of the Greek word *parakletos*[6], which is a compound of two Greek words, *para* and *kaleo*. *Para* means "very close." Paul used this word to describe his relationship with Timothy. *Kaleo* means "to call." This word was frequently used in Scripture when the apostles were describing their callings. The Father called upon the Holy Spirit to take the place of Christ here on earth to abide with the apostles. He would comfort them, lead them to a deeper knowledge of truth, and give them the strength to overcome trials. And to this very day He has enabled believers all around the world to preach the Gospel with power and authority.

What type of relationship did the disciples have with Jesus? They lived, walked, and talked with Him. It wasn't a two-hour-on-Sunday type of life with Jesus. It wasn't a thirty-minute quiet time with Him in the mornings. Following Jesus wasn't the same as following a celebrity on Twitter or your favorite preacher on Instagram. They actually lived their lives with Jesus. They spent days and nights with Him. The disciples didn't pray to Jesus; they talked with Him. They were free to talk with Him whenever they had doubts, questions, or problems. He was their Friend.

---

6   "G3875 - paraklētos - Strong's Greek Lexicon (kjv)." Blue Letter Bible. Web. 29 Mar, 2023.
    https://www.blueletterbible.org/lexicon/g3875/kjv/tr/0-1/.

Today, you can have the same relationship with the Holy Spirit that the apostles had with Jesus. That's why Jesus told His disciples, "I will send another," which, is the word *allos*[7] in the Greek, and means "one besides, another of the same kind." "Another of the same kind" is like when you're in a coffee shop, you order a small latte, and after you're finished, you ask the barista to get you another one. That means another drink of the same kind. The Holy Spirit wants to be to believers today what Jesus was to the disciples back then. That's why He lives in us just as Jesus physically lived with His disciples. The Holy Spirit wants to fellowship with us in the same way that Jesus fellowshipped with His disciples.

The Holy Spirit wants to have this communion with all Christians, not with just a few of us. This is important! The communion of the Holy Spirit is for everyone, not just for the spiritually elite. None of us feel worthy of the Father's love, nevertheless, His grace is undeserved towards everyone. But when it comes to the communion of the Holy Spirit, so many feel like it's only for Pentecostals, Charismatics, or those in the healing ministry or full-time evangelism. If you're thinking that somehow the Holy Spirit's fellowship belongs only to a special segment of the Christian community, Paul dismantled that notion when he wrote:

> *The communion of the Holy Spirit be with you all.*
> **(2 Corinthians 13:14)**

That's so awesome! It means that everyone is included. The Holy Spirit wants communion with you. Yes, you! You are part of that *"all."*

---

7   "G243 - allos - Strong's Greek Lexicon (kjv)." Blue Letter Bible. Web. 29 Mar, 2023. https://www.blueletterbible.org/lexicon/g243/kjv/tr/0-1/.

Don't believe the lie that you aren't good enough, holy enough, or prayerful enough for the Holy Spirit to have communion with you. He already lives in you. Just give Him personal space and time to have communion with you. It's His gift to you. You didn't deserve grace, yet your life was changed by receiving the grace of Jesus. You would never be able to earn God's love, but His love changes you when you receive it. The same is true with the Holy Spirit. Yes, He is holy, but He wants to be in touch with you constantly, He wants to talk with you, and He wants to walk with you. That ongoing relationship will change your life in the same way that God's grace and love changed your life initially.

Having the communion with the Holy Spirit is not an upgrade to one's spiritual life. It's one of the basics for successful Christian living. When I go through a car wash, they ask if I want a regular car wash or the ultimate car wash, which costs more. The same goes with fuel; there is regular 87 and there is 93—super premium. The communion of the Holy Spirit is not premium Christianity. It's not something deeper or higher. It's just normal Christianity! It's not for the super spiritual or excited Pentecostals. The Holy Spirit is not an optional blessing. An ongoing, vibrant relationship with Him is a necessity for every believer. That's why His intimate friendship belongs to every believer. He invites every benefactor of grace and love to partake of this precious union.

Some believers feel that the communion of the Holy Spirit is like the dessert menu in a restaurant. After you are full of grace and love, if you have any more room and are still hungry, then start developing intimacy with the Holy Spirit; but they think they need to be careful not to become weird like some crazy Charismatics. Skeptics say that taking too much of the Holy Spirit is not good for you, like taking too much cake. Well, the Lord Jesus lived a Spirit-filled life, and His disciples couldn't do anything without the Spirit filling them completely. The same goes for me and you. The communion of the Holy Spirit is not only for the super hungry, it's for everyone, just as grace and love are available for everyone.

I wonder how many of us would no longer battle with loneliness and would stop complaining about not having close friends if we would only open up our hearts and enjoy sweet friendship with the Holy Spirit. Perhaps you might start out being one of His fans, but after you start fellowshipping with Him in your heart, soon you will be His friend.

Now you have learned that the Holy Spirit wants to fellowship with you. In the next chapter, I will take you further into how you can start fellowshipping with Him.

More Than Tongues

Communion with the Holy Spirit

The grace of the Lord Jesus Christ, and the love of God, and the communion of the Holy Spirit be with you all. Amen.

(2 Corinthians 13:14)

*O*ur heavenly Father gives us *love*, the Lord Jesus gives us *grace*, and the Holy Spirit gives us *communion*. Most of us think that the Spirit's primary gift is tongues or maybe supernatural power. No, His primary gift is a relationship. He wants to have an ongoing relationship with you. As I have mentioned before, you are fully qualified for that relationship, in the same way you are qualified for the love of God and grace of Jesus. He desires to have close intimacy with all of us, not just with certain special people.

You can't have a friendship with someone if you keep calling them "it." Many people don't have fellowship with the Holy Spirit because they view the Spirit of God as a force instead of a friend. They see Him as a power, not as a Person. Jesus never referred to the Holy Spirit as "It" but always as "He." The Holy Spirit is a Person, a living being with a personality. He is not just a dove, wind, fire, cloud, force, or power. He is not even a feeling. He is a real Person!

The Holy Spirit Has a Body

When you think of the Father, there is a human connection to a person we already know as our own father. When we think of Jesus, we think of Him as a Jewish man. So, when we worship Jesus, we don't think of Him as a lamb or a lion, but as a Person, even though He is portrayed as a lamb or a lion.

But when it comes to the Holy Spirit, many people are confused. They can't have fellowship with Him because they see Him only as a dove, wind, oil, fire, etc. One time, I asked the Lord why He didn't give the Holy Spirit a physical body if He wanted us to have a relationship with Him. His response totally blew me away. He said, "The Holy Spirit does have a body. In fact, He chose yours. Out of all the bodies He could have chosen, He chose yours." Then I remembered the verse that says that our body is the temple of the Holy Spirit. It hit me. Wow! He chose to live and operate in my body! That even changes how I view my body.

You know, whenever someone famous drives a car or lives in a fancy house, or signs a book or album, the value of those objects goes through the roof. I saw on eBay that one guy was selling a car for a million dollars because, at one time, President Barack Obama leased it. The car was no longer just any car; its value was raised due to the fact that Barack Obama used it before becoming president.

Can you imagine how much more valuable you are because the Creator of galaxies now lives in you? He doesn't just use you for a year or two. No, no, no! He chose your body to be His residence. You are His address. The Holy Spirit is a Person and wants to have a relationship with you. By taking up residence in your body, He also raises the value of your body. If you have felt insecure about your physical appearance, you now have a greater reason to not tolerate insecurity and self-doubt. You can now live in thanksgiving to the Lord, not only for creating your body, healing your body, resurrecting your body in the future, and rewarding what's done in the body, but also for choosing to reside in your body right here on earth.

The Holy Spirit is a Person, Not Power

Let's come back to the Person of the Holy Spirit. What makes someone a person? Is it life? No, because trees have life, but they are not persons. A person is a living, mobile being with a unique personality consisting of traits, feelings, behavior, and temperament. A person is a created being with a soul. The soul is the seat of the mind, the will, and the emotions.

The Holy Spirit has a mind. Paul said, *"He who searches the hearts knows what the mind of the Spirit is"* (Romans 8:27). The mind of the Holy Spirit is in union with the Father and the Son, but He is a separate Person of the Godhead.

The Holy Spirit has a will. Jesus told his followers to go into all the world and preach the gospel, but the Holy Spirit prohibited Paul from going to Asia (Acts 16:6-7). When Paul tried to go to another city, the Spirit didn't permit him to go there, either. The Holy Spirit wasn't against preaching in those cities, but He knows everything better than we do and leads us in ways that help us to be most effective for God and His kingdom. God didn't just give us a map, which is the Bible; He also gave us a Guide—the Holy Spirit. The Holy Spirit's will is in union with the Father and the Son.

The Holy Spirit has emotions. The mind, will, and emotions are what give someone personality, thus making him or her a person. Paul exhorted us: *"and do not grieve the Holy Spirit of God, by whom you were sealed for the day of redemption"* (Ephesians 4:30). To grieve the Holy Spirit is to cause Him sorrow. He is not a robot or machine without emotions or feelings. Even though He is described as fire and wind, He is neither of those because fire and wind don't have a mind, will, and emotions. The Holy Spirit is a Person. And our actions can bring Him joy or displeasure.

The Holy Spirit is Not Tongues

In order to talk to the Holy Spirit, we must view Him as a Person. Some see the Holy Spirit as tongues. Therefore, they think that because they speak in tongues, they have all there is to have of the Holy Spirit. Speaking in tongues is a powerful gift that unlocks other gifts, but communion with the Holy Spirit is much more than just speaking in tongues. Speaking in tongues accompanies the baptism in the Holy Spirit. It's a gift, but the Holy Spirit is a Person. No, the Holy Spirit is not tongues; He is God. Yes, it's possible to speak in tongues but not have any intimacy or friendship with the Holy Spirit. It's possible to walk in the gifts and still lack a relationship.

Samson exercised his gift of extraordinary strength but didn't make a close connection with the Spirit of God. Jesus warned His followers of some people who cast out demons, heal the sick, and prophesy, but practice sin and don't know Him personally (Matthew 7:22-24). Relationship with the Holy Spirit must take priority over exercising His power and gifts.

Speaking in tongues should fuel your relationship with Him, but don't view the Holy Spirit as merely speaking in tongues. That's like saying that Jesus is the sinner's prayer. The sinner's prayer leads a person to salvation, but Jesus is God, a Person who is greater than a prayer. The Holy Spirit is more than tongues; He is God. He wants to have a relationship with you. That relationship starts with understanding that you must view Him as a Person, not an "It." He wants to be your friend. Stop treating Him as a force or a mysterious energy. The Holy Spirit is not a power; He is a Person.

The Holy Spirit is an Unnamed Servant

There are many shadows and prototypes of the Holy Spirit in the Old Testament. One of the clearest comes from the story of Abraham, his son, and the oldest manservant in his house.

> So Abraham said to the oldest servant of his house,
> who ruled over all that he had, "Please put your hand
> under my thigh."
>
> **(Genesis 24:2)**

Abraham is considered the father of faith. He had two sons: Ishmael, who was the first son after the flesh, and Isaac, the son of the promise. We could say that God also had two sons: Adam, who represents the flesh, and Jesus, the Son of promise. Just as Abraham offered up his son Isaac and then received him back alive, so was Jesus sent by the Father to die for our sin and then was raised from the dead. Isaac was the heir of the entire estate of his father, just as the Father in heaven gave all authority to His Son and placed everything under His feet.

The oldest servant in Abraham's house was a most trusted servant who was assigned to find a bride for Isaac. Abraham's faithful household servant drew no attention to himself. His attention was focused only on finding a bride for Isaac to fulfill Abraham's wish. In fact, the author of Genesis doesn't even call him by name, in order to keep him in the background. What a beautiful example of the Holy Spirit, who came to earth to draw people to Jesus to be His bride. The Holy Spirit comes to glorify Jesus and to make Him known. He points to Jesus, He speaks what Jesus would speak, and He declares that everything that belongs to Jesus is available to us.

Even though the oldest servant was nameless, he oversaw all that Abraham had. His administrative ability in the household was so outstanding that Abraham trusted him to find a bride for his son. No, Abraham didn't send him to find a camel or a house for Isaac, but a wife. That speaks of enormous trust! He not only ran Abraham's household, but also made important life decision for Isaac. I see a similarity with the Holy Spirit: He manages heaven's resources. Jesus said:

He will take of what is Mine and declare it to you.
(John 16:14)

The Holy Spirit is the Administrator in the heavenly realm. He was there during creation, turning God's Word into reality. God the Father places attention on the Holy Spirit, even though the Holy Spirit doesn't draw attention to Himself. The Holy Spirit is not optional or something extra in the Christian life if we really want to see the kingdom of heaven manifested here on earth. In fact, the kingdom of God is manifested through the Holy Spirit.

For the kingdom of God is not eating and drinking, but righteousness and peace and joy in the Holy Spirit.

(Romans 14:17)

All the operations of the Father and the Son are administered through the Holy Spirit.

Will You Give Him a Drink?

So, this servant-administrator of Abraham's household was now on his way to find a wife for Isaac. He met a young virgin woman by the well, who was beautiful to behold. Rebekah represented the church, the bride of Christ, who is called to walk in purity and drink from the well of salvation. Mind you, this servant had men with him and many camels that carried goods. But he made this request of Rebekah: *"Please let me drink a little water from your pitcher"* (Genesis 24:17). He could have gotten that water from the well himself. He could have asked one of his guys to draw water for him, but here he puts himself at her mercy. Now, we know that this was a test. His thirst was her test. If she would give him water, and water his camels also, she would be the one.

What if I were to tell you that the Holy Spirit is thirsty? Oh no, not like He is dehydrated and wants you to give Him H2O; He is thirsty for your attention. The Holy Spirit waits to be wanted. He desires fellowship with you. He wants you to talk to Him. Yes, Jesus told us that if we are thirsty, we can come to Him and drink of the Holy

Spirit, but if the Holy Spirit is thirsty, can you give Him a drink? Can you hear His sweet voice asking for a drink?

PLEASE indicates a petition, not a command. He doesn't want to force you to fellowship with Him. He is not ordering you but simply asking this of you as a friend.

LET ME reveals the Holy Spirit is God, but He is also a Person who has feelings and affections and longs to be invited.

DRINK A LITTLE, not a lot, not all of it, just a little. Could you give Him a little attention every day? Pause during your busyness. Stop what you're doing, and just acknowledge Him.

FROM YOUR PITCHER—your calendar. We all have the same 24 hours, and our pitcher needs to be refilled every morning. He desires to drink from your pitcher. He wants your attention, your affection. We let everyone else drink from our pitcher; it's time to let Him drink first.

The best thing you can do right now is to stop reading this book; close it and go spend some quality time with this wonderful Person. Develop a daily habit of constant communion with the Holy Spirit. Talk to the Holy Spirit if you desire to walk in the Holy Spirit.

Water the Camels

Rebekah gave Abraham's servant water from her pitcher and then volunteered to water his camels as well. On average, a camel drinks 8 to 12 gallons of water per day. And a thirsty camel can drink up to 30 gallons of water in one sitting. That's a lot. And he had more than one camel. That's a lot of work! But she volunteered; he didn't ask her to do that. I can imagine the scene: the men standing around just watching this young woman carry water for all those camels.

Little did she know that the camels she was watering were holding expensive gifts for her and her family. Everyone wants the gifts of the Holy Spirit, but we must focus first on giving the Holy Spirit our water—our time. Also, we ought to volunteer to water His camels— the local church. Sign up to volunteer at the kids' ministry. Look for a place to serve, not a platform to shine on. Do the work that maybe others don't want to do. The Holy Spirit is watching everything. While others are seeking gifts, you water the camels. You will be surprised how His gifts will eventually flow through you. If you water the camels, He will give you His gifts. As you serve God's cause on this earth, He will empower you with His anointing.

Gifts of the Holy Spirit are not jewelry, but they beautify the life of a believer. Gifts of the Holy Spirit are tools for service to accomplish God's work with God's help. Many people don't have these gifts because they are not passing the test of serving in the local church. The Holy Spirit wants to use us to build His kingdom. Therefore, He will test us first by watching whether we will water the camels or go on begging for gifts so we can show off. Today, so many folks want to use the Holy Spirit to build up their name, ministry, and fame. The Holy Spirit doesn't use them, because they are only seeking to use Him. Focus on watering the camels. Focus on working for the Lord with the gifts and talents you already have. Do the natural; the Holy Spirit will add super to your natural, and you will do the supernatural.

In the next chapter, we will look at the results that will begin to happen to you when you yield to the indwelling presence of the Holy Spirit.

Surrender to the Spirit

Character by the Holy Spirit

But the fruit of the Spirit is love, joy, peace, longsuffering, kindness, goodness, faithfulness, gentleness, self-control.
(Galatians 5:22-23)

*I*n the beginning of this book, I mentioned the story of the lame man at the temple who had legs but didn't walk on them. Believers can be the same way: having the Holy Spirit but not walking in the Holy Spirit. To walk properly, you must have the use of both legs available. Both legs have to be the same length and be functional. The same applies to our walk in the Holy Spirit. We must have two legs, and they are equally important: the fruit of the Spirit and the gifts of the Spirit—character and charisma. There are nine gifts and nine characteristics of the fruit of the Holy Spirit.

A life full of the Holy Spirit has both character and power. Jesus was the perfect example of that. He was the most Spirit-filled Person that has ever walked on earth. He was full of love but also of power. Jesus sought to reproduce in His disciples both the heart of the kingdom and the ability to walk in the power of that kingdo

We are exhorted to *"not quench the Spirit"* (1 Thessa and to *"not grieve the Holy Spirit"* (Ephesians 4:30). Quenc when we limit His power. Grieving takes place when we ignore His promptings and act contrary to His character. When you quench the Holy Spirit, you don't allow His power to flow. When you grieve the Holy Spirit, you don't allow His presence to produce the fruit. The Holy Spirit wants to empower our lives with His anointing and equip our character with His fruit. I call this the two legs of walking in the Holy Spirit.

As I've mentioned already, we need both His fruit and gifts just as an airplane needs two wings. The anointing will take a person to higher places, but character will keep that person from becoming proud and then crashing when he is at the top. The Holy Spirit is both wings of the same plane. He is the Giver of gifts but also the Producer of the fruit that we call character.

The Fruit of the Spirit

There are nine gifts of the Holy Spirit, but one fruit of the Spirit. It's interesting because Paul doesn't call it nine fruits of the Spirit; he names nine characteristics and calls them the fruit.

> *But the fruit of the Spirit is love, joy, peace, longsuffering, kindness, goodness, faithfulness, gentleness, self-control.*
> **(Galatians 5:22-23)**

Why is it fruit and not fruits? These nine character qualities of the Holy Spirit come at the same time. This fruit is what He develops in our character throughout our lifetime. In our own strength, we can work on only one trait of the fruit of the Spirit at the expense of the others. When we work on patience, we tend to lose sight of gentleness.

Or if we get better at long-suffering, we may lose joy. That would be our best effort; but without the Holy Spirit, we can't develop the entire fruit of the Spirit at once. It's hard to remember all nine attributes of the Spirit, and that's why this is called the fruit (singular) of the Spirit.

It's not the fruit of my own efforts. It's not my work. If this would come as a result of my achievements, it would be called the fruit of personal efforts, not the fruit of the Spirit. Before describing the fruit of the Spirit, Paul writes about works of the flesh. The works of the flesh are plural, but the fruit of the Spirit is singular. It's worth to note that all those evil works he mentions are connected with the flesh, not the devil (Galatians 5:19-21). That means there are two approaches to character formation: the flesh or the Holy Spirit—works or fruit. Maybe the problem with our character is that we are working on it in our flesh instead of letting the Holy Spirit produce those qualities by a continuous surrender to His indwelling presence.

Surrender, Not Striving

Fruit is not developed by striving. Trees don't struggle to produce fruit. Branches simply abide on the tree and they bear fruit. It's your surrender and abiding that the Holy Spirit will use to produce His character in you. It's your attachment to the Holy Spirit that brings fruit. Therefore, you don't work on your fruit; you work on developing a close relationship with Him, and fruit comes as a result. Again, that's why it's called the fruit of the Holy Spirit, not the fruit of your efforts.

This may come as a shock to some, but we are not called to work on developing our character. We are called to work on our relationship with the Holy Spirit, and He will work on our character in return. Jesus told his disciples, *"Follow Me and I will make you..."* (Matthew 4:19).

Their assignment was to follow; His assignment was to make. Even though Jesus addressed different character flaws in His disciples, it was their abiding with Him that changed them over time. This same promise remains today: if we follow the Holy Spirit, abide in Him, and develop communion with Him, He will make us into good, patient, loving, joyful, kind, faithful, gentle, long-suffering and self-controlled people. At the end of the day, all the credit will be His, not ours.

We are only branches. Our part is to abide; His job is to produce fruit. That's why John 15:1-8 says that a branch *bears* fruit, not *produces* it. We only hold on to that fruit, but the Holy Spirit produces it. Our job is to cultivate intimacy; His job is to produce character. In other words, don't focus on your issues; instead, cultivate a close relationship with Him.

Even though fruit does take time to develop, it's the abiding in the tree that brings it to maturity so it's ready to enjoy. Time alone doesn't bring fruit—abiding does. Flavors take time to mature. Only the Holy Spirit changes our character with time. Healing, deliverance, and salvation are instant, but sanctification is a process brought forth by the Holy Spirit.

Let the Spirit Live Through You

Remember, God is interested in spiritual fruit, not religious nuts. Life filled with the Holy Spirit is not you making an effort to live for God, but letting the Holy Spirit live through you. Paul said, *"It is no longer I but Christ who lives in me"* (Galatians 2:20). We receive salvation when we believe that Jesus died in our place on the cross, but do you know how character is developed? It results when you surrender to the Holy Spirit and give Him total access to your heart, soul, and body! Yes, let Him live His life through you.

Salvation came when Jesus died in our place, but sanctification comes when we let the Holy Spirit live His life in us. Of course, it's easier for most of us to recognize that Jesus died for us than to allow Him to live in us. That second part requires surrender. It is surrender that allows for the fruit of the Spirit to be produced in us.

Having the fruit of the Holy Spirit is like having kids; children are the result of intimacy. Many people come to the altar for the pastor to lay hands on them in order to have a better character. You know that someone laying hands on you can't get you pregnant. You can't get fruit because you came to the altar. Just like in physical life, you need to have a marital relationship and intimacy, and kids come as a result of that. The same is true of His character in us; it's a fruit that follows intimacy.

Attitude, Not Just Actions

It's interesting that all nine characteristics of the fruit the Holy Spirit develops in us are attitudes, not actions: love, joy, peace, longsuffering, kindness, goodness, faithfulness, gentleness, and self-control. These are not issues of behavior but of attitude. If you remember, the Ten Commandments are all about doing this or not doing that. But the fruit of the Spirit is not about doing, but being. It's not about action, but attitude. What is an attitude? John Maxwell[8] wrote:

> Attitude is the librarian of our past, the speaker of our present and it is a prophet of our future;

---

8   John Maxwell is an American author, speaker, and pastor who has written books primarily focusing on leadership. www.maxwellleadership.com.

its roots are inward, but its fruit is outward; it is our best friend, or our worst enemy; it is more honest and more consistent than our words; it is an outward look based on past experiences; it is a thing that draws people to us or repels them from us.

In other words, attitude is more about our reaction to what's happening around us. Most of the time, how we react to situations in life is more important than the situations themselves. Why is the Holy Spirit more concerned with our attitude than our actions? Because your attitude determines your altitude in life. The fruit of His working in your heart is a change of your attitude toward life. We tend to think that His number one job is to change circumstances so that we don't have to change our attitude. We pray that He will change other people, so we don't have to change. But the Scriptures teach us otherwise.

That's why I believe that the fruit of the Holy Spirit doesn't make me better than you; it makes me better than me. It empowers me to do what I can't do on my own.

Fruit Feeds

Fruit doesn't feed itself; it nourishes others. When you let the Holy Spirit produce His fruit in your life, the people closest to you will be fed by you. Your spouse, family, and friends will be nourished by the quality of your character that has been influenced by the Holy Spirit.

The gifts of the Holy Spirit bring healing, deliverance, and salvation, but the fruit of the Holy Spirit brings nourishment. If you have only gifts but no fruit, the people closest to you will starve. Your gift touches the world, but your spouse is fed by your character. At home, your anointing is not as important as your attitude. At work, your co-workers are fed by the fruit of the Spirit in you.

Gifts operate on the stage, but fruit feeds people at home, school, and work. My wife admires me as a preacher, but she loves me as her husband. Being a good preacher can't make our marriage great. I must allow the Spirit to produce the fruit of being a loving husband. Otherwise, I will become one of the statistics of pastors committing adultery or seeing their marriages fall apart. In these cases, it's not their gift that is struggling, but their fruit.

Fruit feeds. If we don't have fruit, people around us will be fed up *with* us. If we have fruit, people close to us will be fed *by* us. So, let's be honest, are people fed up *with* you, or are they fed *by* you? You might be very gifted and anointed, but are you fruitful?

If you have an unbelieving spouse or parents, they don't care how great your church is. They want to know how great your attitude is toward them. Many of us fail to bring them to Christ because we are only pursuing gifts, and we don't let our family get fed by the fruit of the Spirit. What if your household was fed every day by the fruit that the Holy Spirit has produced in you? Most of them would be open to the gospel.

There are pastors who are famous worldwide, but their kids don't want to talk to them. Why? They have gifts and anointing, but their family is hungry for love and attention. They are longing for fruit.

You can't feed your kids with an Apple watch, but you can feed them with an apple fruit. Your gift is like an Apple watch, but the fruit of the Spirit is like the apple fruit. I don't want to own the coolest Apple watch but deprive my family of being fed by the fruit because

I am so busy working on my gifts that I neglect to allow the Spirit to work on my character.

Fruit Grows

Fruit grows. It grows slowly. Sometimes it is sour before it is sweet. It's a process. The fruit of the Holy Spirit is no different. You can't get His fruit at a conference or during revival services. It doesn't come through the laying on of hands. It can't be received as a gift; it must grow as fruit!

It's not instant. Nobody can impart the fruit of the Holy Spirit by the laying on of hands. You can do that with the gifts but not with fruit. You can get an anointing like that but not a change in your character. It will take time.

By the way, time doesn't change your character; it's the Holy Spirit who does that—though it does take time for Him to change us. This process will not be fast or accelerated. No matter how great your gifts and anointing are, the fruit of the Holy Spirit will take time. Like Warren Buffet said, "You can't produce a baby in one month by getting nine women pregnant."[9]

Fruit takes time. It grows slowly.

How does it grow? I am reminded of a scene in the movie Evan Almighty, in which Morgan Freeman plays God. This scene really helps to understand how the fruit of the Spirit grows. Evan's wife prays for the family to be closer, and her husband claims to have heard God tell him to build a ship. She is embarrassed by him, so she takes the kids and leaves him. In the restaurant, as she is waiting for her food,

---

9   *Minimalist Quotes,* minimalistquotes.com/warren-buffett-quote-15753/.

Morgan Freeman, who plays God, comes to her and asks, "If someone prays for patience, do you think God gives them patience? Or does He give them the opportunity to be patient? If they pray for courage, does God give them courage, or does He give them opportunities to be courageous?"

God gives us the fruit of the Spirit in seed form; He then provides us with opportunities for that fruit to mature as we choose to lean on the Holy Spirit in those moments. The more we yield to the Holy Spirit in times of fear, the more the fruit of faith is developed. As we surrender to the Holy Spirit in times of stress, the fruit of longsuffering is cultivated. When we have an opportunity to get offended but we depend on the Holy Spirit, He develops the fruit of love. Don't for a moment think that the fruit of the Holy Spirit will come automatically. The Lord will give you an opportunity, and you will have to choose to lean on the Holy Spirit, not on your flesh.

Sometimes when I act out of character, my attitude shows up. But I give myself grace and remind myself that my fruit of patience, for example, is still sour, and that the Holy Spirit is not done with me. I am still under construction. As I abide in Him, He will not leave me nor forsake me until He develops fruit that glorifies Jesus.

Christian character will not be developed by striving but by surrendering. Surrender to the Holy Spirit. Stop trying harder; try differently. Start yielding to the Holy Spirit daily. Yield to Him the areas of your character that are weak and cause you to fail. Whenever a temptation presents itself for you to act out of character, at that moment, follow the Holy Spirit away from sin. You will sense His prompting; don't grieve Him by ignoring His whisper.

*Walk in the Spirit, and you shall not fulfill the lust
of the flesh.*

(Galatians 5:16)

In the next chapter, we will look at how hosting the Holy Ghost privately will drastically change your life publicly.

Hosting or Hiding?

Continuing with the Holy Spirit

Chapter 6

*But you, when you pray, go into your room, and when
you have shut your door, pray to your Father who is in
the secret place; and your Father who sees in secret will
reward you openly.*

(Matthew 6:6)

I want to tell you a story about two different people. Both
accounts come from the Old Testament and provide a sharp
contrast in behavior that I will use to describe our relationship
with the Holy Spirit. Two stories. Two different people.

- One was hiding some*thing*, and the other was hosting some*one*.

- One faced certain doom, and the other had a promising future.

- One was a soldier, and the other was a prostitute.

- One destroyed his family, and the other saved her family.

- One brought defeat to the nation, and the other was used to
save the nation.

You have probably figured out who I am talking about: Achan and
Rahab. These stories happened in the book of Joshua chapters 2, 6

& 7. While their stories happened around the same place and time, these individuals couldn't be more different from each other. Both were hiding something, but *what* they were hiding forever changed their lives.

Hiding Sin

God specifically told Israel not to take anything from Jericho after they conquered it but to put it under a curse and bring total destruction to the land. All gold, silver, and bronze were to be put into God's treasury. However, Achan disobeyed God's command; he took forbidden objects and hid them underground beneath his tent.

Achan's story represents those who publicly look like soldiers but privately live as slaves to the passions of lust and their greedy flesh. The problem wasn't so much with his sin, but with the fact that he hid it and didn't confess until he got caught. Sin loves secrecy because sin always grows in the dark. Maybe you are like Achan, living publicly in the promised land of salvation, going to church, staying away from the "obvious sins" that could land you in jail or cause your license to be suspended, but privately, you are hiding secret sins. There is a difference between privately struggling, battling, fighting, praying, fasting, and confessing your sins, as opposed to living in sin, enjoying it, hiding it, and getting better at not getting caught. In the same way, there is a huge difference between a sheep falling into the mud and a pig playing in the mud. The sheep will cry in the mud and struggle to get out, but a pig loves the filth and enjoys it. If you are fighting privately, my goal is not to guilt-trip you. Sin already does that. But I want to remind you that hiding and living in secret sin will make you spiritually inept or unfruitful. The only hope is to bring your sin out of the tent and into the light of truth.

I myself once lived a double life like Achan. As a teenager, my secret sin was pornography. It made me sick, guilty, and ashamed. I had feelings of worthlessness and hypocrisy. I felt trapped by the passion of the flesh. However, one thing that I knew the devil could not do was to control what I did *after* I fell. Would I hide my sin like Achan? Would I hide like Adam in the garden? Or would I bring it to Jesus, confess it to my mentors, and seek help?

I chose to not hide my sin, and I did not wait to get caught. I ran to God and to my pastor to confess it. Even as a teenager, I knew that the conviction of the Holy Spirit was enough motivation to confess. I think the reason Achan continued to hide the forbidden objects in his tent was that the Israeli people had experienced a huge, miraculous victory in the city. The enormous walls of Jericho had just fallen down, and the inhabitants were being eliminated. He probably felt as though that kind of victorious breakthrough was a stamp of approval on his life. Oftentimes, breakthrough, success, and even God's favor can be perceived as God's approval on our lives, in spite of the fact that we are hiding in our sin.

Because the sentence against an evil work is not executed speedily, therefore the heart of the sons of men is fully set in them to do evil.

(Ecclesiastes 8:11)

In other words, if our sin is not punished right away, we feel as though we can keep on doing it.

Secret Sins Become Public Scandals

Please understand that miracles happening in your life or through your ministry are not signs that you are in the center of God's perfect will.

> *On that day many will say to me, 'Lord, Lord, did we not prophesy in your name, and cast out demons in your name, and do many mighty works in your name?' And then will I declare to them, 'I never knew you; depart from me, you workers of lawlessness.'*
>
> **(Matthew 7:22-23)**

Seeing healings and deliverances is not a sign that God is pleased with you. One of the biggest mistakes a leader can make is to assume that because the ministry is growing, the finances are flowing, and their reputation is glowing, that they are right with the Lord. They may be taking new territory for God, but if what's hidden in their tent is displeasing to the Lord, then they are not right with Him. If you are not in His secret presence, privately pursuing a pure heart and living out God's principles when no one is watching, you can be sure that miracles, signs, wonders, victories, and breakthroughs are no proof that you are in right standing with the Lord. Sooner or later, what's in your tent will become public, and it will lead to your destruction.

One of the reasons the devil wants you to advance in the kingdom while living in sin is so that when you fall, not only your life and reputation will be destroyed, but the lives of all those around you will be adversely affected as well. The more you succeed while living in secret sin, the worse you will harm yourself and hurt others. If you fall from a one-foot elevation, you probably will not die. However, if you fall from the third story of a building, you will meet a tragic fate. The longer you keep your gold, silver, and Babylonian garments hidden, the more it will affect you and the people connected to you. If Achan would have confessed his sin right away, then 36 other soldiers would not have died in the battle against the neighboring city of Ai. His sin destroyed him, his family, and many others as well.

Sooner or later, whatever is hidden will be revealed. Private secrets become public scandals.

For nothing is secret that will not be revealed,
nor anything hidden that will not be known and
come to light.

(Luke 8:17)

Don't wait until you get caught. Don't postpone your repentance until you get arrested. Don't ignore the Holy Spirit by holding on to secret pleasures that will become your lasting pain and embarrassment. You don't need to get fired from your job to get a wake-up call. Remove whatever you're hiding under your tent before you get removed from the ministry. Confession is better than getting caught. Confession of sin follows the conviction of the Holy Spirit.

Sin is not worth hiding. Period. Don't struggle secretly or suffer silently. Bring that forbidden thing into the light! I don't mean post it on Facebook or Instagram, or message some "man of God" on social media who has no idea who you are, and spill all your beans to him. That's weak and cowardly. Take it to the cross—to Jesus. When you have sinned, don't hide from God—run to Him. Follow up your confession to God by going to your spouse, a trusted mentor, a pastor, your mom, or your dad. Going to someone to open yourself up will cause your heart to beat faster and your blood to rush. It takes courage to get real and raw. Then you will see how God will not only cleanse you but free you from the pull of that forbidden fruit, your secret sin.

If we confess our sins, He is faithful and just to forgive us our sins and to cleanse us from all unrighteousness.

(1 John 1:9)

Hosting Spies

Enough about hiding sin. If you have spent any time in church or in a religious circle, you may have heard all about sin and its consequences. So, I don't want to focus too much on sin. The story that fascinates me more than Achan hiding his sin is the parallel story of a woman hiding two men in her house.

Rahab wasn't exactly the woman of the year. Let's just say her profession was less than commendable. Many would say she was a mess and a hopeless case. On top of everything, she was living in the wrong place at the wrong time because her city was marked for total destruction. However, upon hearing rumors about the mighty acts of God in Egypt, and then encountering the Hebrew spies, she decided to bring them into her place and host them. Not long after that, officers came from the king searching for the spies and she was faced with a choice: hide the undercover agents or expose them. She made the right choice and hid them. That act of hosting the spies completely changed her life.

Achan's hiding things ruined him, but Rahab's hosting the two spies changed her life for the better. She and her family were saved from total destruction. But it doesn't end there. Rahab went from being a prostitute to being the wife of Salmon, one of the spies she hosted. Not only that; she also became the mother of Boaz, who became the father of Obed, who became the father of Jesse, who became the father of King David, and the rest is history. She is even one of the only five women mentioned in the genealogy of Jesus. That's pretty special. Hosting two men of God changed this woman's life. It was not only the act of inviting the spies into her home, but hiding them. She was rewarded for not giving them up when the city officials demanded that she reveal their whereabouts.

Pain Fuels the Pursuit

I can relate to Rahab. No, I haven't worked in the sex industry or lived in Jericho, but for a long time, I felt like I was born on the wrong side of the tracks. Because of a delivery mishap during my childbirth, the upper eyelid on my left eye is now weak and droopy. When I look up, my left eye doesn't move up either. That's no problem when you are a kid, but when you grow older and into your teenage years where peer pressure, name-calling, and bullying come into play, it hurts. It hurts badly. The enemy used all of that to feed my mind with lies that I was worthless, inferior, and my life amounted to nothing.

I was convinced that there was plenty of evidence in my physical appearance to confirm those lies, and I had a hard time fitting in with the crowd. I wasn't very good at anything, no matter how hard I tried. I consistently felt rejected in places where I desperately wanted to be accepted. On top of all that, I was in a new country without friends and not knowing the language or culture. My emotional pain was joined with physical pain. I had excruciating headaches every summer; it seemed like no amount of pills would take them away. I started to entertain thoughts that this world would be a better place without me. I wanted to escape. I wanted to run. I honestly wanted to disappear.

But pain pushed me to the prayer closet. I would close myself in my room after school and cry out to God. Most of my prayer time was spent complaining, pouring out my bitter soul to God. I felt like I was dumping out my emotional and physical pain in prayer, only to be filled with pain again the very next day. As I shared my teenage heart with God in prayer, I felt more and more peace. This peace began to pass all understanding, but nothing on the outside changed. Prayer became my coping mechanism. Soon it became a habit. I didn't pray to get inspired for a sermon, find power, or to be more spiritual. I was simply hurting. His presence became my healing. Little did I know that God would use that "secret place" to change me.

As His presence became more and more real to me, my insecurities started to fade. The more I became profoundly aware of Him, the more I lost sight of myself. The same body, the same eyes, but a different perspective. Externally, my life began to take a turn. The little bit of ministry that I did in the church started to get other people's attention. With my broken English, I started to get invitations to speak at Christian clubs in school. One thing led to another, and my ministry to the Lord in my secret place birthed ministry to the world. On the outside, I am still the same guy today; but on the inside, the Holy Spirit has transformed me.

I am a living testimony that hosting the Holy Ghost in private will change your future. There are many believers whose only goal is to get free from their secret sin or to stop hiding the bad things they've done. That's a good step in the right direction, but it's not the final destination. By avoiding secret sin, you may avoid shame, guilt, and scandal, but that alone will not change your life. Even if your private life is void of sin but not full of the Holy Spirit, your years to come will remain unchanged.

If the devil can't get you to hide your sin, he will try plan B, which is for your private life to be full of busyness and neglect of prayer. If you no longer hide your sins but don't host the Holy Ghost, you are still susceptible to this trap of the enemy. It could be just living an empty life, without meaning, focusing primarily on the cares of this life and on the deceitfulness of riches, pleasures, and selfish ambitions.

Private Disciple, Public Reward

In his first letter to the Corinthians, the apostle Paul exhorts us to build our spiritual house on Jesus Christ as its foundation. We should use gold, silver, and precious stones so that on the day of judgment, our work will endure and we will receive God's reward. On the other hand, if we build with wood, hay, and straw, then the fire will burn it and we will suffer loss, even though we ourselves will be saved in the end. So, every Christian is building on the same foundation but using different materials. The six types of materials that Paul mentioned can be put into two categories. Gold, silver, and precious stones are in one category. Wood, hay, and straw are in the other.

Gold, silver, and precious stones are found underground.
Wood, hay, and straw are found on the ground.

Gold, silver, and precious stones are expensive.
Wood, hay, and straw are cheap.

Gold, silver, and precious stones are rare.
Wood, hay, and straw are common.

Gold, silver, and precious stones are in small quantities.
Wood, hay, and straw are in large quantities.

Gold, silver, and precious stones are purified by fire.
Wood, hay, and straw are destroyed by fire.

Well, there we have it. These are the two varieties of materials that we can use in building our Christian life on the foundation of Jesus Christ. Is our building material found underground? Does it cost us something? Is it rare, small, and purified by fire? Or is it found on top of the ground? Is it cheap? Is it common and available in large quantities, but will be destroyed by fire?

In Matthew 6, when Jesus addressed the issue of the believers' disciplines in life, He corrected three things: giving, fasting, and prayer. It is interesting that He talked about the motives behind giving, fasting, and prayer and attached a reward to each of them when done right.

Hmm. What if giving is like gold, fasting is like silver, and prayer is like precious stones? They are all found underground when done for the right reasons. They are practiced in secret, but they're something that God sees openly. Giving, fasting, and prayer cost us some personal sacrifice. Believing in Jesus costs us nothing, but following Him costs us everything we have. This type of living is rare. Unfortunately, most believers don't live a life of sacrifice, personal devotion, and self-denial. Their spiritual life is just common, ordinary, and average. This is snowflake Christianity, which is fragile, weak, carnal, and easily offended. It's inflated with self-discovery; it's like a balloon—all it takes is a needle of discomfort to deflate it. When this sort of life is refined by trials and tribulations, it pops and explodes with a bang.

Gold, silver, and precious stones aren't afraid of fire. When your private life is deeply rooted in obedience to the Holy Spirit, not only can you withstand the tests and trials of life, but you can also be positioned to receive rewards and approval from God. God rewards publicly what's done in private. I truly believe that God will reward and honor us here on earth, but the real reward is the recompense we will receive when we eventually face the judgment seat of Christ.

Host the Holy Ghost in private. Take much time to talk with Him in prayer. Dive deep into His Word. Obey His promptings. Flee sinful environments and situations. Keep your mind pure. Guard your heart with all diligence from offenses and resentment. Yes, your progress may be slow and small in the eyes of man, but you are building your spiritual life with imperishable materials.

The alternative to hosting the Holy Ghost is living in compromise: settling for a lukewarm relationship with God, living in a complacent state of self-approval, talking the talk but not walking the walk, making promises but never living them out, and living as close to hell as possible without going there. That's life on the fence: trying to get just enough of God to miss hell and just enough of the world to miss enjoying God. Wood, hay, and straw; that's all it is. A carnal life is an unrewarding life. Sure, you may still miss hell, but you will also miss all you were called to be and to enjoy as a believer. It's time to upgrade your building materials. It's time to clean up the garbage from your private life and fill it with precious gold. Dear ministers and leaders, wood, hay, and straw are abundantly available but result in nothing more than busyness. We are not called to be busy, but fruitful. Fruitfulness is the primary result of intimacy and abiding in the Holy Spirit.

> *He who abides in Me, and I in him, bears much fruit; for*
> *without Me you can do nothing.*
>
> (John 15:5)

People have become more obsessed with becoming popular rather than being pure. It's easy to build with wood, hay, and straw and neglect your private life with God. With natural gifts and skills, we can do big things for God; but effective, fruitful Christian life and ministry are different from a business in the sense that they flow out of a close relationship with God.

God is looking at your personal life today. He sees what's in your closet, in the drawer, under the bed, or behind the couch where no one else looks. He is looking for something to reward publicly. Will He find something in your secret place that will be worth rewarding publicly? Are you fasting without anyone knowing it? Live in a secret place of giving, fasting, and prayer, and your Father in heaven will reward you openly. He will openly honor you.

Consistency is the Key

We are invited to host the Holy Ghost who lives here on earth. The earth is His. Rahab was living in the land that was promised to Israel, and she hosted the spies who entered the city. In the same way, the Holy Spirit enters our hearts through an invitation, which results in salvation. But through surrender we enter into an ongoing intimacy with Him. Salvation invites the Holy Spirit into your life, but surrender initiates a close companionship with Him.

In other words, the Holy Spirit comes when we receive Jesus as our Lord and Savior, but our relationship with Him grows as we host Him. He wants to be wanted, longs to be invited, and desires to be hosted. Rahab didn't just notice the two spies that were in the city; she hid them in her house. Not only did she hide them, but she made every effort to not surrender them to the soldiers who questioned her. Likewise, we need to make a consistent effort to maintain an ongoing relationship with the Holy Spirit.

But many of us have a huge problem. We begin a closer relationship with God after reading a book or going to a conference, but then give up a few weeks later due to busyness, distractions, the demands of life, or responsibilities at work. Others give up hosting because they become lazy, indifferent, and just don't "feel like it" anymore. Rahab didn't give up, even when she was pressured to do so. She protected those she hid. Little did she know how much that would change her life. Nobody knows what the Holy Spirit is able to do when we host Him and pay the price of being consistent.

Consistency is the key. Work hard at cultivating your secret place with God. That's one of the ways that God helped me to develop spiritually in my early years: the habit of taking much time to be in His presence. Many people don't see results from abiding in His presence because they quit too soon. They spend time with the Holy Spirit for a month or two and then stop. They find something more important to do. Imagine if Rahab would have done that; the spies would never have changed her destiny. You have to make spending time with the Holy Spirit a priority every day. Frankly speaking, you can always find time to do the things you really want to do. Create a plan and fight procrastination or anything else that tries to steal your time with the Holy Spirit. Create a routine for your own personal revival.

Revival is not a one-time event; it's a lifestyle. It's not just about having some big moments with God, but also developing momentum with Him. Some people love going higher with the Lord, but then they don't cultivate a lifestyle that supports a continued pursuit after Him. Push through laziness, plow through procrastination, and develop the habit of constantly living in His presence. You have no idea how that will change your life!

In the next chapter, we will explore the leading of the Holy Spirit. Learning to discern the voice of the Holy Spirit will become much easier after you read that chapter.

The Secret of Being Led by the Holy Spirit

Connection with the Holy Spirit

Chapter 7

For as many as are led by the Spirit of God, these are sons of God.

(Romans 8:14)

 esus Christ modeled the best version of a Spirit-filled life, and He invites us to imitate Him in the way that we live.

- Jesus was born of the Holy Spirit.

- Jesus was filled with the Holy Spirit.

- Jesus was led by the Holy Spirit.

- Jesus was anointed by the Holy Spirit.

- Jesus did miracles by the Holy Spirit.

- Jesus offered Himself as a sacrifice by the Holy Spirit.

- Jesus was raised from the dead by the Holy Spirit.

- Jesus breathed the Holy Spirit on His disciples.

- Jesus asked the Father for the Holy Spirit to be poured out.

- Jesus baptized believers into the Holy Spirit.

You can see that the Holy Spirit played a major role in the life of Jesus. Jesus fully depended on Him and defended Him in front of others. Obviously, we can't give the Holy Spirit to someone, nor can we pray to the Father to send the Holy Spirit anywhere on earth—that has already been accomplished. But everything else, like being born again, filled, led, anointed, and empowered by the Holy Spirit, is possible for all believers today. Jesus didn't just depend on the Holy Spirit for Himself; He promised to give us the Holy Spirit. He didn't want His followers to do anything without first being empowered by the Holy Spirit. In fact, John the Baptist called Jesus "the Baptizer in the Holy Spirit." He immerses us into the Person, power, and purpose of the Holy Spirit.

In the example of Jesus's life here on earth, we see the progression of our own relationship with the Holy Spirit. For example, before we can be used by the Holy Spirit, we have to be led by the Holy Spirit. Before we can be led by the Holy Spirit, we must be filled with the Holy Spirit. Before we are filled with the Holy Spirit, we must be born of the Holy Spirit. If there are steps to growing in the Holy Spirit, it would be safe to say that these are the steps: be born of the Spirit, filled with the Holy Spirit, led by the Holy Spirit, and then used by the Holy Spirit.

Supernatural Life Starts with Supernatural Birth

Jesus's earthly relationship with the Holy Spirit didn't start with miracles, signs, and wonders. It began with His birth.

Now the birth of Jesus Christ was as follows: After His mother Mary was betrothed to Joseph, before they came together, she was found with child of the Holy Spirit.

(Matthew 1:18)

Jesus was born of the Spirit. His life on earth was supernatural because His birth was supernatural. Our own supernatural life is the direct result of a spiritual birth. The Scriptures call this *the new birth* or *being born from above* (see John 3). In order to be led by the Holy Spirit, we have to first be born of the Holy Spirit.

Flesh gives birth to flesh, but the Spirit gives birth to spirit.

(John 3:6 NIV)

When we are born into the natural world, we are born with physical eyes and ears. With eyes we see the world, and with ears we can hear it. During our second birth, we are born with spiritual senses—with spiritual eyes and spiritual ears. Our spirit man, the real us, can be in contact with the spirit world. The Bible tells us, *"For as many as are led by the Spirit of God, these are sons of God"* (Romans 8:14). Being led by the Holy Spirit comes naturally to those who are children of God. Little children don't need to go to school to hear or see; their natural birth gives them that ability. Training helps them to understand what they hear. Schooling helps them to make sense of what they see. But the ability to hear and see comes with birth. So it is with spiritual birth.

And the sheep follow him, for they know his voice. Yet
they will by no means follow a stranger, but will flee from
him, for they do not know the voice of strangers.

(John 10:4-5)

Sheep know the voice of their shepherd. The first prerequisite
to hearing God's voice is being one of God's sheep who follow Him.
You must be born again into God's family. You have to be His child.
Your spiritual rebirth makes it natural to hear the voice of the Holy
Spirit and to obey.

But as many as received Him, to them He gave the right
to become children of God, to those who believe in His
name: who were born, not of blood, nor of the will of the
flesh, nor of the will of man but of God.

(John 1:12-13)

You've Got to be Filled
Before You are Led

Then Jesus was led up by the Spirit into the wilderness to
be tempted by the devil.

(Matthew 4:1)

Then means right after the events that occurred in Matthew 3:13-
17, which narrates the baptism of Jesus, during which the Holy Spirit
came upon Him like a dove. Right after being filled with the Holy Spirit,

Jesus was led by the Spirit into the wilderness. Note the progression: leading follows filling. After Jesus was filled, He was led. This happens naturally because we will be led by whatever we are filled with.

If we are filled with selfishness, we will be led by selfishness. If we are filled with anger, we will be led by anger. If we are filled with offense, we will be led by bitterness. But if we are filled with God's peace, joy, and righteousness—which is what being filled with the Holy Spirit is—then the Spirit of God will guide us. God's nature and character will be on full display in our lives. So instead of seeking God's leading, we should focus on being filled with God. The Spirit of God leads those who are filled with Him. Remember, being led by the Holy Spirit is the mark of sonship.

I also want to note that the Holy Spirit *leads* us; He doesn't *drive* us. We drive a car, but we lead sheep. We are not a means for the Holy Spirit to meet a goal for Himself; we are not a method for Him to reach a destination. We are precious to Him. He leads us into the Father's purposes and plans in the same way a shepherd leads his sheep into green pastures. He leads us through Bible meditation, inner promptings, the still small voice, through common sense, the counsel of others, circumstances, and sometimes even through divine signs.

People frequently ask me, "How do you know it's really the voice of God?" or "How do you discern the leading of the Holy Spirit?" I think it's simple. When you spend time with Him and walk in total submission to the Holy Spirit, His leading comes naturally; you learn to hear His voice more clearly. So, the question shouldn't be, "How do I hear the Holy Spirit?" but, "How can I stay closer to Him every day? How can I stay full of Him, not only during the times when I need clear direction, but all the time, as a lifestyle?"

There have been times when I was in the living room and my wife was in the next room, separated by a wall, and I would ask her something. Often, she wouldn't hear me, not because I didn't speak, but because she was too far away. She would ask, "What did you say?" So, I would say it louder, but she still couldn't hear the question. Until we came closer together, she couldn't understand what I was saying. If you can't hear the Spirit, don't fret and worry; just focus on being filled with Him, because whatever you're filled with will lead you.

On my journey with Him I also learned that the Holy Spirit doesn't like to scream; He whispers. That's why you must be close enough to hear those whispers. When my wife and I are in the same room, I don't have to yell or speak loudly; I can speak quietly because she is close to me. If the Holy Spirit has to scream for you to hear Him, it means you're too far from Him. He whispers because He wants closeness and intimacy.

Relationship Before Revelation

Relationship *with* the Holy Spirit is more important than revelation *from* the Holy Spirit. Getting insights from God concerning our future is only secondary; finding Him to be our primary Source of peace, joy, and stability is the most important thing. The Holy Spirit will share His secrets with those who find Him to be the Source of their strength and spiritual abilities. He will guide you without fail if you make Him your Comforter when all other comforts fail.

David, anointed to be the next king of Israel, was rejected by the Philistine army commander, who refused to allow him to engage in battle against Israel. When David and his 600 men returned home, they found that their little town had been burned down by the enemy, and their wives and children had all been taken captive (see 1 Samuel 30:1-6). Of course, this situation is appalling, and I wouldn't wish it upon my worst enemy. David's rag-tag band of men wanted to kill him because of their overwhelming grief. David was greatly distressed! What I find fascinating in this story is that David first went to God to get "inner strength" before He asked God for further directions. David first strengthened himself in the LORD, and then He inquired of the LORD.

This is the key to hearing the voice of God: put greater emphasis on seeking God's presence in your life before you ask Him for anything. Being strengthened first by the Lord is the key to hearing the voice of the Holy Spirit. When your emotions are all over the place, or your heart is broken, or your mind is bogged down with problems, you'll find that your spiritual receptors aren't working too well. One of the quickest ways to get into God's presence is through praise and thanksgiving. It's best to go to God first to find His peace and comfort by praising Him before asking Him for directions.

As I've mentioned already, at the time when David was super distressed, he turned to God for internal strength. However, his rival, king Saul (his father-in-law), who was going through his own struggles on the battlefield, had a totally different approach to problems.

When Saul saw the army of the Philistines, he was afraid, and his heart trembled greatly. And when Saul inquired of the LORD, the LORD did not answer him.

(1 Samuel 28:5-6)

Do you see the difference in King Saul, who was trembling with fear? He desperately went to ask God for direction instead of going to God for inner strength. Saul didn't have much of a relationship with God to begin with.

Throughout my life, I've realized that when I face difficult situations, I often panic and get overly desperate and impatient to get answers right away. When I do that, I lose a sensitive discernment of God's voice, fall into deception, and end up in defeat. Everyone is prone to do that. God did not speak to Saul, nor even acknowledge him, so he went to a witch for a "word on demand." He got a word, but he never got the solution he desperately needed. Saul and his three sons died that very day in the battle, as he'd feared.

Friends, let's learn from these examples. Allow the Lord first to fill you with His presence if you want Him to lead you. Allow the Holy Spirit to comfort you and strengthen you in the inner man if you want Him to guide you out of the situation that you are in. If you are oozing toxic waste due to anger, offense, confusion, or bitterness, you need God's healing before you can discern God's leading. Perhaps fear, doubt, and anxiety are overwhelming your soul; strengthen yourself in the Lord first, and then set your heart to hear what He will tell you to do.

My wife has been trying to get me to take vitamin supplements. She bought a box of pills with unfamiliar chemical names, and I had to take three to four tablets daily. One morning, right after I awoke, I gulped them down and within a few minutes, I threw up. All the vitamins came out. It was a bad experience. You probably have guessed that my issue wasn't with the vitamins but with taking them on an empty stomach. You can't take medicine on an empty stomach. And so it is with seeking the Holy Spirit's leading; don't do it on an empty soul. Don't be like Saul, who was filled with fear and sought to get immediate direction from the Lord. Be like David, who went to the Lord first to be strengthened, and only then did he inquire of the

Lord. Go to God to build intimacy within your spirit before you go to God to inquire of Him.

The Holy Spirit Leads Where the Flesh Doesn't Want to Follow

Let's go back to the leading of the Holy Spirit in the life of Jesus. What comes as a surprise is that the first mention of Jesus being led by the Holy Spirit was into the wilderness, into fasting, and into temptation—in other words, into a battle (Matthew 4:1-11). The Spirit didn't lead Him to preach, heal, or deliver, but into the wilderness and into fasting! When we get baptized in the Holy Spirit, we will begin to hear His promptings, but they don't usually lead us where we want to go or tell us what we expect to hear.

The Holy Spirit leads us to pray, fast, humble ourselves, ask for forgiveness, extend forgiveness, give sacrificially, and serve without grumbling—things that make our flesh complain. Most people, in fact, would ignore or question that kind of leading of the Holy Spirit because they are so addicted to comfort. Then they wonder why He doesn't speak to them, and how to hear His voice above the surrounding noises. In reality, they don't want to listen to God; they want God to speak what they want to hear—and there's a huge difference between those two things.

Following the Holy Spirit means denying the flesh. It means a detachment from material things and carnal interests. It usually involves giving up something good for something even better that God has waiting for those who are obedient. Do not be surprised if hearing God's voice begins with something that will cost you. But, if you ignore that voice, you mute and grieve the Holy Spirit. It's like muting audio on the computer; the sound is still coming, but you can't hear it because the computer is on mute.

I remember when I felt prompted to give away all my financial savings for the first time; I rebuked that thought! I had plans for my savings; they were supposed to go toward a down payment on the house we wanted to build. It didn't fit into my mental box how my good God could ask for such a huge sacrifice like that from me. But, when I decided to take the risk, it required every ounce of faith on my part. Here's the secret I learned: hearing God always requires faith to listen. When I did what the Holy Spirit prompted me to do, I saw God take me through the wilderness and then into the promised land.

Today, after many years of heeding the voice of the Lord, I have gained more and more experience, but it still requires much faith on my part to obey God. God's voice usually leads to a sacrifice before it takes us to success. Ignoring the promptings of the Holy Spirit only grieves the Holy Spirit. It will dull our faith because we missed the chance to stretch it. Oh, how much we miss by not following the Holy Spirit!

It is Written

We live in a generation today where many Christians say: "God told me to leave the church." "God told me to marry this person." "God said…" and "God told me this and that." Yes, I believe that God does speak to us today through His Word and through His Spirit. What concerns me is the lack of declarations such as: "It is written," and I hear more the over-emphasis on "God said…" or "God told me…" Let me explain. In the garden of Eden, Satan questioned what God had said; Eve responded with what God did say, although she added an extra phrase. Both Adam and Eve heard God's voice, and they tried to live their life based on that voice. But when Satan tempted Jesus in the wilderness, Jesus quoted Scripture and boldly declared, "It is written." I am pretty sure Jesus could have muttered, "God said." Being the Son of God, He could have even replied, "I said." Instead, He proclaimed the Holy Scriptures. He defeated the tempter with these words: "It is written."

If you want to get familiar with the voice of the Holy Spirit, get filled with the written Word of God. If you can't get a personal word from God, get into the Word of God. Meditate on your Bible day and night, and it will become a part of you. He is in His Word. Jesus is the Word of God.

Earlier, we mentioned how God didn't speak to King Saul when he was in desperate need of a word from God for direction. I think this is why:

> So Saul died for his unfaithfulness which he had committed against the LORD, because he did not keep the word of the LORD, and also because he consulted a medium for guidance.
>
> **(1 Chronicles 10:13)**

Did you notice that? He didn't keep the Word of the LORD. If you don't keep God's Word, why should He give you another word? If you want to hear the voice of the Holy Spirit, give proper honor to the sword of the Spirit, which is His holy Word. The Bible is His book. If you keep the Word of God in your heart, you will keep the voice of God in your spirit.

God's voice never contradicts His Word. To recognize His voice, we must get to know His Word. I advise young preachers to avoid saying, "God told me" in every other sentence throughout their sermon, but to replace it with, "It is written." Sadly, some people today add "God told me this or that" to everything that comes to their mind. Get anchored in God's Word if you want to be familiar with His voice.

Heeding the Voice of Yesterday

Each time the Holy Spirit asks us to do something and we don't do it, we will hear from Him less and less. In fact, disobedience to the voice of the Holy Spirit can surely mute His voice in our hearts. It's not so much that He stops speaking to us, but we become deaf to His voice by choosing to not obey it. We become hard of hearing.

When God didn't speak to Saul anymore through dreams, prophets, and Urim, he went to a medium to conduct a séance and conjure up the prophet Samuel, whom he expected to reach God for him. When the witch entered the spirit world to bring Samuel up, Saul complained to the spirit about how God had left him and didn't want to talk to him anymore. The spirit said the following shocking words:

> *Because you did not obey the voice of the LORD nor execute His fierce wrath upon Amalek, therefore the LORD has done this thing to you this day...tomorrow you and your sons will be with me.*
>
> **(1 Samuel 28:18-19)**

In other words: *Saul, you stopped obeying the voice of the Lord, and therefore He has stopped speaking to you!*

The reason you can't hear Him today is because you stopped heeding Him yesterday. Yesterday's disobedience affects today's hearing. If you find yourself in the same place as Saul, go back to the last thing the Holy Spirit told you to do and do it. Repent and obey. That act will unmute His voice in your life. You don't deserve a new word if you haven't obeyed the old one.

And hearing God's voice doesn't make you more spiritual; it's heeding His voice that makes the difference. Notice one important thing: seeking to hear God's voice makes you totally accountable to obey that voice. You don't get off the hook after you hear His voice. Ignoring that voice puts your future contact with God at risk. The voice of God is the key to your breakthroughs, but the keys that you don't insert into the lock—*and turn*—are simply pieces of metal. If you want to go into the next room of your life, you need to use those keys that have been given to you.

Four Voices

There are four main voices that you will need to recognize or discern from each other: God's voice, the devil's voice, people's voices, and your own voice (or the voice of your soul). Adam and Eve heard the **voice of the LORD** daily and knew the sound of His voice. God clearly instructed them to not eat from the Tree of the Knowledge of Good and Evil, and as long as they obeyed His voice, they lived in paradise. They enjoyed God's company. Obedience to the voice of the Lord is the key to friendship with Him.

You are My friends if you do whatever I command you.
(John 15:14)

The same thing applies to intimate friendship with the Holy Spirit: it is reserved for the obedient. If you want to be friends with the Holy Spirit, it's more about obedience than just simply hanging out with Him. What made Adam and Eve commit their vile, grievous sin is not that they stopped hearing God's voice; it's that they stopped obeying His voice.

The second voice you might hear is the **voice of the devil**. His voice is very different from the voice of the Holy Spirit. In the garden with Eve and in the wilderness with Jesus, the devil introduced doubt concerning God's Word. It's clear that the devil didn't physically hit Eve or attack Jesus with his fists. His strongest weapon was (and still is) his sneaky voice trying to create doubt about what God had said. He is a deceitful liar and shoots fiery darts into your mind—intrusive thoughts. He is devious, conniving, unethical, and immoral. Like a snake, he attacks through his teeth with venom. He uses his mouth; his words are his strongest weapon. Though he is not a lion, he roars like a lion; someone has said the devil is a mouse with a microphone. His sly voice condemns, discourages, confuses, frightens, and induces stress, but God's voice gives loving conviction, encourages you, clarifies, reassures, and brings you peace. When the devil speaks, his words always produce worry, hurt, and despair, which is in sharp contrast to the Holy Spirit, who brings kind words of comfort, healing, and hope.

The devil's voice comes in the form of intrusive, tormenting, blasphemous, and improper thoughts. Thoughts of suicide, fear, lies, lust, and vulgar imaginations are not just your flesh working against you—they are him speaking because he constantly tries to steal, kill, and destroy. You can be sure that whatever causes doubt and contradicts God's character is devilish. You can silence that evil voice by using your authority and commanding the devil to get out of your life. Go ahead, drive him crazy by quoting truth from Scripture or praising God right in his face. That will give him a headache, and he will leave you.

The third voice we hear, and often follow, is the **voice of other people**. Adam got into trouble when he obeyed the voice of his wife. Eve listened to the voice of the serpent, and Adam listened to the voice of Eve. God cursed the ground because Adam gave ear to the voice of his wife instead of obeying the voice of God. Just because she was his disobedient wife, Adam didn't have to blindly follow her and disobey, too. As her husband, he should have rebuked the snake and led his wife away from that tree, instead of following her suggestion to eat the forbidden fruit. The devil doesn't have to speak to us directly to get us off track. He very often uses other people to speak wrong ideas or thoughts into our minds.

What about the internet, social media, television, wrong friends, or immoral magazines? Of course, we do have to socialize with people, but we must always respect God's Word and authority above all. Ask God for discernment, and do not take everything that people say to you as good advice, or you might find yourself deceived and defeated. Remember, King Saul lost his anointing by listening to his people who were complaining to him. He should have led them to victory, but instead, they pressured him to disobey God. When Jesus was on earth, the people who were living in Israel under Roman occupation wanted to make Him their king, but He didn't give in to their wishes. Peter expected freedom from Roman tyranny; he did not want Jesus to die on the cross, but Jesus rebuked the devil out of Peter. Later, when the same Peter was filled with the Holy Spirit on the day of Pentecost, he boldly followed in the steps of Jesus. When religious leaders told him to shut up and not talk about Jesus, he refused to obey them.

Satan often uses certain people as his agents to put you under their control, manipulation, and domination. It's a form of witchcraft. If he can't get to you by speaking directly to your soul, he will use others around you to cause hurt, pain, and pressure to get you off track. Don't yield to them; follow Jesus. This doesn't mean that we shouldn't listen to people, ask their advice, or submit to our elders; but, when they contradict what God has called us to do, we must obey God's voice. Jesus, who overcame the devil's voice in the wilderness, had to contend with the devil's voice through people close to Him: *Don't die, Jesus! Become our king! Come down from the cross!* Do you know who was doing the talking? Were they just people giving their ideas to Jesus about His ministry? Of course not. It was the devil using people to try to get Him off track. We need discernment as never before; otherwise, we will end up trying to please people instead of obeying God.

The last voice is our **own inner voice,** which we must distinguish from the voice of the Lord. The devil's voice is easier to discern because we know it's always contrary to the Word of God and in total opposition to God's character and nature. Our own voice is much more difficult to distinguish from the Lord's. A lot of times, our own personal thoughts will seem like the voice of the Holy Spirit. People often say, "Let your conscience be your guide." But we must test the spirits; we shouldn't believe everything that comes to our minds. Our natural heart is deceitful above all things; we shouldn't trust it, but instead trust in God (see Jeremiah 17:9).

While we shouldn't be critical of everything we think, we can't be naïve either. When I personally started listening for His quiet voice, I would get impressions in my spirit of what I thought the Holy Spirit was saying to me. I took risks in trusting that it really was the Holy Spirit speaking. When I perceived that my thoughts were in line with the Word of God and with His heart concerning such things as giving money, sharing the gospel, or giving a specific word to someone, I started to take small risks, and my confidence in hearing God's voice grew. Seeing the fruit of obedience to that inner voice made me more assured that I was not hearing my own voice but the voice of the Holy Spirit. Sometimes I got it wrong, and I was quick to acknowledge that! What helped me most was to not rush into anything right away but to keep that word, or idea, in my heart for twenty-four hours as I pondered and examined its motive and biblical basis. As a married man, I also consulted my wife, requesting her to pray as well and confirm that word. I still do these things today.

We know that God very often speaks through His Word by high-lighting certain Bible passages that directly apply to our life as we meditate on the Scriptures daily. He also speaks through a still small voice that comes in the form of a thought, an impression, intuition, or just common sense. God speaks to some people through pictures in their minds. We also know that God speaks through visions and dreams. Dreams happen during the night and visions during the day. Also, prophets, pastors, and those in spiritual authority are channels through which the Holy Spirit speaks today. There are other ways, such as a rare audible voice or trance. God is very creative and knows how to get our attention! The most important part on our end is to humbly incline our ear to hear Him.

Appointing Without Anointing

The Calling Without the Holy Spirit

Chapter 8

'Not by might nor by power, but by My Spirit,' says the LORD of hosts.

(Zechariah 4:6)

The story of Saul started out really well. Occupied with his father's business, Saul was looking for the family's stray donkeys. He wasn't looking for a kingdom or a title that day, but destiny found him when he was on a journey to fulfill his dad's assignment. When we engage ourselves in doing our heavenly Father's business, destiny will find us. When we are looking for lost souls, we will not miss our divine calling.

Saul had a calling in his heart to lead a kingdom, even as a little boy. It was God who placed that desire in him. When he met the prophet Samuel to inquire about the wandering donkeys, Samuel told him that he would reveal to him the next day what was in his heart, but also assured him the donkeys had already been found (1 Samuel 9:19-20). Donkeys were on Saul's mind; destiny was in his heart. Samuel told him about the donkeys right away, but he waited until the next day to tell him about the calling of God.

So often, when God places dreams in our hearts—even if they are radical or crazy—we are afraid to admit to ourselves that those dreams are present and real. But God has a way of pulling them out from the back of our minds. True prophetic ministry doesn't just show us our faults, but reveals our destiny. The prophet disclosed what was in Saul's heart. His calling to rule over Israel was confirmed with the anointing of the Holy Spirit, who enabled him to fulfill God's dream for his life.

Your appointing requires anointing. A calling can't be fulfilled without anointing. Saul wasn't called to be a preacher or worship leader; he was called to be a king, but anointing was required for success. God gives the anointing of the Holy Spirit to those whose task is greater than their ability. When God gives you a dream that seems not just hard, but impossible, He will equip you with the proper tools to fulfill it. Your anointing enables your appointing.

Let's look at the role of the Holy Ghost in your calling and then contrast that with what happens when the anointing no longer influences your life. King Saul was a perfect example of this.

Attacking or Attracting?

The anointing is an overflow of God's life within us. Our cup goes from full to overflowing. When we walk in the Holy Spirit, He causes our cup to run over into the lives of others. The anointing is the result of walking in intimate fellowship with Him. The writer of Hebrews said that because we love righteousness and hate wickedness, God anoints us more than others.

Therefore God, Your God, has anointed You with the oil of gladness more than Your companions.

(Hebrews 1:9)

Saul didn't have to seek God's power for his life; the anointing sought him when he walked in sync with the Spirit of God. The anointing enabled him to break the yoke of the Ammonites at the beginning of his reign. But when he stubbornly continued disobeying the Lord, the anointing left him, and he started to fight not the enemy, but God's anointed men. He went from humbly attracting God's anointing to attacking God's anointing in others. He spent the latter part of his life trying to kill his son-in-law, David, who portrayed what Saul had once been—filled and led by the Holy Spirit.

One of the clear-cut signs that Christians are not walking in the Holy Spirit is displayed when they pick at other believers. There are those who create revivals, and there are those who criticize them for their efforts and methods. Those who find fault with revivals don't create them. If you criticize God's move and His Spirit moving in others, it's because He's not moving in your own life. If He were allowed to move in your life, you would be busy with God's projects, and you'd work together with others instead of attacking them.

David didn't attack King Saul; he had his own personal anointing to maintain. But Saul constantly attacked David because the anointing in his own life was gone. All men and women of God have faults; the ones in the Bible had sins and weaknesses just like the ones God uses today. Honoring the Holy Spirit in another person doesn't mean that we ignore their humanity or turn a blind eye to their shortcomings. But, if you make it your job to degrade others simply because you don't agree with their style, accusing them of heresy because you don't agree with manifestations, you must examine your heart. Or maybe you envy the favor that others walk in. If so, you need to take a deep look into your own heart and ask yourself, "Has the sweet, manifest presence of the Holy Spirit in me been smothered or quenched?"

Dear friends, we can disagree with someone without trying to destroy them. We Bible-believing, Jesus-following, Spirit-filled saints are all on the same team! When we attack anyone who is being used by the Lord, not only do we miss out on God's blessed anointing, but we are also in danger of even grieving or blaspheming the Holy Spirit. This topic of blasphemy was brought up in response to Jesus being called a devil for casting out a devil in the name of the devil. The religious Pharisees didn't say anything against the Holy Spirit; they credited the exorcism and healing to the devil, even though it was clearly done by the power of the Holy Spirit! Blasphemy against the Holy Spirit has very little to do with what we might foolishly say about Him; it has much more to do with what we say against His works, which are obviously accomplished by Him. Blasphemy is ascribing to demonic powers that which was performed by the Holy Spirit.

I urge you to avoid speaking against miracles, especially against operations of deliverance done by Christian ministers you do not like. Yes, there are false miracles, false prophets, and false everything else. For everything real and godly, there will be a counterfeit. The devil is a duplicator; he is a copycat. However, God is the one and only almighty Creator with total authority in the spirit realm. Satan misused Scripture when tempting Jesus in the desert, yet Jesus fought back by quoting Scripture. Satan abused the Scriptures, but that does not mean we should be reluctant to use the Bible in our defense. In Egypt, the magicians performed miracles by the power of magic and demons, but Moses didn't try to persuade Pharaoh just by talking and using kind words; instead, Moses demonstrated the supernatural power of almighty God through even greater extraordinary manifestations.

Today, everyone has an opinion about everything. That's fine. However, accusing folks of being heretics or giving the devil credit for miracles and deliverances in other ministries is borderline blasphemy.

There are miracles done by witch doctors, prophecies by psychics, and a focus on angels and energy by New Age cults, but that shouldn't make us avoid the Holy Spirit and His supernatural manifestations. Jesus acted outside of the religious norm; He broke many religious rules and traditions of that day. As a result, the Pharisees labeled Him demonic. When they couldn't discredit the validity of the miracles they witnessed, they accused him of having a demon. The "Pharisees" of today are the same: they glorify "the Moses" or the religion of yesterday, but discredit the Christ of the New Testament in action today. In other words, they talk about revivals of the past, but attack the present-day, contemporary, supernatural moves of God. As a result, they have a form of godliness but deny the power of God (2 Timothy 3:5). This grieves the Holy Spirit.

Men and women of God are not perfect, but that doesn't give us the liberty to call them heretics; they are human beings whom God is using. We have no right to say that Satan is the source of the manifestations occurring in their ministries; it is God who approves or disapproves. Ministers of God are like gloves—God is the hand. Gloves get old, dirty, and worn out, but the Hand remains the same. The people God has used throughout history had their problems too, much like the gloves in your house, yet they were the best tools that God had available at that time. I wish that Noah who got drunk, Moses who murdered, David who committed adultery and murder, and Solomon who practiced idolatry, had not committed those sins; but despite their shortcomings, they were still used by the Holy Spirit. You can read in the Bible about their feats of faith and what they accomplished. If you *attack* miracles, you will not *attract* miracles because that attitude grieves the Holy Spirit. When you do, it is clear evidence that you are not abiding in the Holy Spirit.

Let's return to the story of Saul. He attacked David after he lost his connection with the Holy Spirit. He lost his authority to attack the real enemy and, instead, he made an enemy out of God's chosen person. He convinced himself and others that David was a traitor when, in reality, Saul was just living without the Spirit's power.

Courage or Cowardice?

When the Holy Spirit, through the prophet Samuel, anointed and appointed Saul to be king, boldness was released into Saul and he acted with borderline recklessness. He killed his oxen and sent a very strong message to the people of Israel. He became decisive, bold, and courageous. However, years later, the Holy Spirit left Saul because of his disobedience; he became paranoid, scared, and acted like a coward (1 Samuel 16:14).

When we are full of the Holy Spirit (totally surrendered), we are filled with boldness; but when we are controlled by our self, we will remain normal or balanced. People who lead balanced lives do not change history or make big impacts on the world around them. It's those who step out in faith, take risks, and are bold who are remembered and who impact the world.

There was a time in my life when I was balanced when it came to healing. I didn't want to appear crazy or radical. I was afraid of getting criticized. I believed in healing, but I also believed that God was not willing to heal everybody. Guess what? I wasn't being criticized, and nobody was getting healed. But as I started to get closer to the Holy Spirit, His presence became more important to me than the approval of man. The pain of sick people became more important than the opinions of healthy people. I started to notice a new boldness in my prayers, preaching, and teaching. That boldness brought on a greater measure of the movement of God. Healings in our ministry then became a regular event. Intimacy with the Holy Spirit will lead you to take risks, and those risks will lead to great rewards.

During the time when King Saul was playing it safe—waiting forty days for Goliath to make the first move—David came onto the scene. Without military experience or a prophetic word to fight a giant, he threw himself into the battle against Goliath. David had what Saul had lost—boldness. He wasn't stupid or reckless. David had a relationship with the Holy Spirit. A relationship led to risk; risk led to reward. Saul didn't value his relationship with the Holy Spirit, so he paid the price—he lost his boldness. He became balanced. He lost his courage and became cautious. He lost his faith because he was playing it safe.

Now, let's focus on the Holy Spirit, not on risk-taking. If you try to imitate someone else who is walking in the Holy Spirit without nurturing your own relationship with Him, you will not take risks; though, you could become reckless, and your recklessness could lead you into ruin. You might remember that when Israel refused to go and take possession of the promised land soon after leaving Egypt, God became angry with them. He said that none of them would enter into the promised land. All those who were twenty years old and older would die in the desert, except for the two courageous spies. Well, after hearing God's declaration, they became reckless and went ahead without a proper relationship with Him. They didn't seek direction from the LORD and engaged themselves in battle, getting whipped by their enemy as a result (see Numbers 14). Without a living relationship with the Holy Spirit, our attempts at boldness are reckless, which leads to nothing but destruction.

When you hear of someone's feats of faith, rejoice, but don't try to copy them. Imitate their faith but build up your own. If you copy someone else's acts of faith instead of imitating their faith, you will fail miserably. When the Egyptian army copied Israel by going through the Red Sea, they drowned, even though Israel had just preceded them on dry ground. Why? Because trying to reproduce someone else's accomplishments of faith, without getting the faith that enabled them to produce those works, will lead to nothing but catastrophe.

There is a difference between risk and recklessness. Risk is born out of a trusting relationship; recklessness is born out of impetuous desperation, impatience, and a need to prove oneself. For example, three times over the past six years, my wife and I gave all our money away, and one time we gave not only money, but our cars as well. We ended up without a car and without money. I truly felt that God had led me to do that. I had been developing a sensitivity to His voice, slowly but surely, and not long after that huge sacrifice, everything in my life and ministry turned around. In fact, I believe that what you see today in my life is a result of that huge risk. But a word of caution: it would not be wise for you to copy me. The key is not giving everything away; the key is having an intimate relationship with the Holy Spirit and living in obedience to Him. Most likely, He will lead you to do something different than me. Just obey!

In fact, at the beginning of the year 2020, not knowing what would come later that year, I felt led to go in a completely different direction: to save money, invest, and teach our church to do the same. The year before, in 2019, we had encouraged everyone to make a huge financial sacrifice in the church; but in 2020, I told the church that God wanted us to learn not only to give but also to save money and invest wisely. Little did I know that COVID-19 was around the corner. My wife and

I still give more today than before, and our church not only survived the pandemic, but grew, and we acquired new property.

I truly believe that my advice and counsel were inspired by the Holy Spirit. There's no formula for acquiring direction; it's entirely about having an ongoing relationship with the Holy Spirit, and nothing else. This relationship will lead you to courageously step out of your boat. Your relationship will lead to risk. Risk will lead to reward.

Now when they saw the boldness of Peter and John, and perceived that they were uneducated and untrained men, they marveled. And they realized that they had been with Jesus.

(Acts 4:13)

Religious leaders saw in the disciples, whom they had thrown into prison, something interesting—boldness. The apostles were courageous. Where did this courage and boldness come from? A college degree? A title and position? Political connections? Personality traits? Not really! Luke, who wrote the book of Acts, told us the secret: the religious critics saw their boldness and realized that *they had been with Jesus* (Acts 4:13). Peter and John were not trying to be fearless. They were just best friends with Jesus, and boldness came as a result.

I believe that intimacy with the Holy Spirit is the key to boldness. And boldness is the key to miracles. Someone who leads a balanced, calculated life will not dream of stepping out and praying for someone to be healed. But someone who has the boldness that the Holy Spirit gives, will step out and pray for healing. Or the boldness to walk on water. Or the boldness to sacrifice. Or the boldness to cast out demons. Or the boldness to share their faith with a stranger. If you don't step out and take a risk, there's no chance for success. Stop playing it safe! Get into your secret place, develop intimacy with the Holy Spirit, and then step out and live in the faith zone.

A result of intimacy with the Holy Spirit is boldness; without it, there is dread, paranoia, fear, and panic. King Saul wasn't just a coward; he became emotionally unstable. He became demonically oppressed. In fact, he became mentally unbalanced. We forget that there is no neutral spiritual ground. There is either light or there is darkness. If we turn off the light in a room, we don't have to invite darkness; it comes without invitation. Darkness fills the room the moment light leaves. That's how anxiety, phobias, and worry show up. When light is no longer there, darkness remains. When the Holy Spirit stops being honored as the Lord of our life, darkness will linger in some shape or form. One of the motivations for developing a profound intimacy with the Holy Spirit should be our concern for what life would be like without Him. We must consider where that would lead. It would lead to the same situation in the room when we turn off the light—total darkness. The extent that we reject the Holy Spirit's leadership in our lives will be the extent to which we will be filled with darkness, apprehension, anxiety, or depression.

Fear of God or Fear of People?

When the Holy Spirit came upon Saul as king, the fear of God came upon the people. His courageous act of killing his oxen and dispatching dismembered parts of the animals to all the tribes sent a strong message to the people, but it didn't scare them—it brought the fear of God upon them. If Saul had been hostile or cruel, the people would have been afraid of him. Instead, Saul's act of boldness, inspired by the Holy Spirit, brought the fear of God, and fearless courage, upon the people. The people began to fear God, not their leader or their enemies.

When people are afraid of their leaders, it's a sign that the leaders are not walking in the Holy Spirit. The Holy Spirit inspires the fear of the Lord, not the fear of pastors (Isaiah 11:2). The Holy Spirit inspires people to walk in the fear of God, not in the fear of man. To fear God is not the same as being afraid of God. Instead, the fear of God causes us to run toward Him and run away from sin; but feeling intimidated by God causes us to run away from Him and hide. The fear of the Lord is having an attitude of awe, reverence, and high respect for Him, holding Him in utmost esteem and admiration. Sadly, we live in a generation today when many believers say they have a relationship with God, but they lack reverence for Him, even using His name in vain. Neglecting one's relationship with the Holy Spirit results in the absence of awe of God's holy presence.

That's what happened to Saul. After his second act of open disobedience, the Spirit of God left him. Then, instead of the people fearing God, they became afraid of their king. And guess what? Saul was afraid of the people as well.

> *Then Saul said to Samuel, "I have sinned, for I have transgressed the commandment of the LORD and your words, because I feared the people and obeyed their voice."*
>
> **(1 Samuel 15:24)**

After the Spirit left him, the decisions Saul made were based on his fear of the people and what they demanded. When Saul was filled with the Holy Spirit, he didn't fear what people thought or said about him because he was focused on God. But when Saul took his focus off God, he became controlled by popular opinion. The fear of man led Saul to give in to their clamor. His focus shifted and he lost sight of God.

When we blindly seek to please people, sooner or later, we will disobey God. When we faithfully obey God, we will serve people without trying to please them. Remember, God didn't ask us to please people, but to love and serve them—and there is a big difference! Jesus didn't live to please people, but to please only His Father in heaven. If we are not filled with an awesome respect for God, then the fear of people will intimidate us. The Holy Spirit creates in us the fear of God. The Holy Spirit doesn't cause us to fear people or fear being rejected by them.

But God has not given us a spirit of fear, but of power and of love and of a sound mind.

(2 Timothy 1:7)

The fear of man won't overwhelm us when we are filled with the Spirit because the fear of the Lord displaces all other fear. If we are walking in the Holy Spirit, those within our circle of influence will be inspired to walk in the fear of God as well. If we don't walk close to the Holy Spirit, we will live in the fear of man. Period.

Authentic approval comes from God our Father, not from men. If we merely love people in the world around us out of pity for who they are, our love for them will dwindle. But if the reason we love them is because we can see them through God's eyes—with His plan and purpose for them—our love for them will grow and be established. The Holy Spirit pours God's love into our hearts for people.

Anointing and Authority

When the Holy Spirit came upon Saul, he went to war alongside the prophet Samuel. This was the message he sent to the nation of Israel:

Whoever does not go out with Saul and Samuel to battle,
so it shall be done to his oxen.

(1 Samuel 11:7)

The king partnered with the prophet. They had a great spiritual relationship as long as Saul was walking in the Spirit. When Saul started to disobey the Lord, it disheartened Samuel greatly and created a conflict in their relationship. Saul began to have issues with authority.

We can't walk in the anointing and oppose authority at the same time. Compare David with Saul. David, who was filled with the Holy Spirit, respectfully did what his father had requested of him and took food to his brothers who were on the battlefield. David didn't go with the intention of fighting Goliath; he only went to run an errand for his dad. But upon his arrival, he heard the giant mocking God's almighty name, and that infuriated him! He consequently asked the timid king for permission to fight the roaring giant. David honored the king's authority enough, although it was weak and deficient, to request his permission to engage himself in combat with the foe (1 Samuel 17).

David then became famous, was drafted into the king's army, and destroyed thousands of Israel's enemies; but he never raised his hand to harm Saul who had been anointed with oil by Samuel. David had also been anointed by the same prophet and had a calling to fulfill, but the jealous King Saul made his life a living hell. One time, David, quietly under the cover of darkness, cut off a part of Saul's garment to later make a point that he did not intend to hurt him. But even that act of cutting off a small piece of Saul's robe brought repentant conviction into David's humbled heart (1 Samuel 24:4-6). David honored authority, even when authority didn't honor him. That's the mark of a life full of the Holy Spirit. Saul had serious problems exercising his God-given authority after he was no longer walking with the Holy Spirit.

Living filled with the Holy Spirit will cause you to change your attitude toward your parents, spouse, pastors, mentors, and bosses. You can't rebel against authority and walk in the Holy Spirit simultaneously. That's not the mark of the Holy Spirit; it's the devil's influence. The devil is a rebel. When we are not influenced by the Holy Spirit and a person in authority gives orders, there is usually some level of rebellion that rises up inside of us. We must not give place to the devil in our lives and should sincerely repent. Pride and rebellion are what got Satan kicked out of heaven. Remember, the devil didn't get kicked out of heaven for doing drugs or watching porn—the reason he lost his position was entirely due to his pride and disdain for God's authority.

Most of us are on the alert for committing sins that would land us in jail, create a public scandal, get us kicked out of church, or remove us from leadership. However, we tolerate and justify the sins that got the devil kicked out of heaven, such as entitlement, unchecked ego, and inflated self-esteem. Pride is at the root of most authority issues.

Our own Savior, Jesus Christ, submitted to His earthly parents long before He began walking in the power of the Holy Spirit. Walking under the covering of authority comes before walking in an anointing. Remember that! The reason God wants us to submit to godly authorities is to develop our character and to prepare us to live under His authority. How can we walk in submission to God, whom we can't see, if we're not willing to walk in submission to the authority we can see?

Our attitude toward authority reveals more about us personally than it does about them. People make excuses for their bad attitude when they don't consider the authorities in their life to be worthy of honor. They say, "Look at what they did or said." Well, our honor for them doesn't demand honor in return from them; we just have to be honorable. It depends on our attitude, not on their actions. But I want to be clear—this doesn't mean that we blindly follow our parents and pastors against the revealed will of God. In that case, we would be disobeying God's authority. Or, if there is abuse or spiritual harassment by spiritual authorities that would wound our soul or create a loss of our personal identity, then we are encouraged to distance ourselves from abusive authority. David did that with Saul. When Saul was throwing spears at him, David distanced himself—but he didn't dishonor Saul. He moved out of the palace and became a fugitive in remote places. But withdrawing himself from King Saul didn't cause him to hate or rebel against him. Remember, distance and disrespect are two different things.

It's our injured ego, inflated self-worth, and pride that lie at the root of our dishonor toward authority. When Noah got drunk, one of his sons dishonored him, and that brought a curse upon him. It's crazy because in the New Testament, Noah is seen as a righteous man, but his son who dishonored his father is considered evil. On our "sin-scale," drunkenness is worse than disrespect toward parents, especially when they are not living up to our standards. Most of us avoid getting drunk, but disrespecting authority is just a normal part of life, or so we think. But what we don't realize is that it can bring a curse upon us.

When we walk in the Holy Spirit, we are willing to honor authority, even if that authority is flawed. When we see the shortcomings of our parents, leaders, employers, or government, we must learn to cover them in prayer instead of criticizing them through gossip or social chit-chat. Just keep your opinions to yourself. If those flaws are committed by leaders in the church, when appropriate, talk to them privately in a spirit of love, meekness, and grace.

Moses's sister, Miriam, spoke out against him for what she considered a good reason—Moses had married a foreigner. It was contrary to the culture of the Hebrew people to marry someone outside of their clan. So, Miriam felt justified in criticizing her brother as a hypocrite. Besides that, she and her brother Aaron envied Moses for his position of leadership. After all, he was younger than both of them. But God didn't see it like that. Instead, the anger of the Lord was aroused against them, and suddenly Miriam got covered with leprosy. She was leprous for seven days as punishment for her critical attitude (see Numbers 12). This story has always messed with me because I always thought it should have been Moses who got leprosy. But God operates in higher ways and in a different realm than we do. The lesson I learned is that I must honor authority—even when I consider them flawed—because my attitude of honor reveals more about my personal character than their defects.

One of the Ten Commandments says to honor your father and your mother. It doesn't say to honor them only if they are nice Christians. It doesn't say to *obey* your father and mother, but to *honor* them. Obedience is different from honor. Obedience is about action; honor is about attitude. Obeying your parents in the Lord is the right thing to do, but honoring them brings reward (Ephesians 6:1-3).

I also want to point out that we must honor law enforcement officers and our government officials. The apostle Peter said,

Show proper respect to everyone, love the family of
believers, fear God, honor the emperor.

(1 Peter 2:17, NIV)

Was it easy to honor the ruthless, cruel emperor? Are you kidding? The guy who was killing Christians? The early church lived with this mindset that honor shows more about their character than about the decadent morality of those they were required to honor. Nowadays it's terrible to see our youth, rebels, and demonstrators calling the police "pigs." How shameful to hear adults calling the president of our country all kinds of derogatory names. And then they wonder why their kids don't respect or obey them. If we sow dishonor, we will reap disgrace. The Holy Spirit doesn't honor this kind of attitude. In fact, if we do not honor or if we have very little respect for authority, it's a sign that we are not filled with the Holy Spirit.

Two of the books that have shaped my understanding of authority are *The Tale of Three Kings* by Gene Edwards and *Under Cover* by John Bevere. I have tried my best to honor and obey my parents as well as my pastor. I'm not going to lie—at times, honoring my pastor was hard. Yes, he was my mentor, but my ego sometimes saw him as my tormentor. My conceit and insecurity got in the way. When my ministry started to grow, my pride also started to grow as I began to receive more and more invitations to speak. I became more and more frustrated with the things that my pastor would say. I am very embarrassed to admit that I felt like I had outgrown my need for my pastor. I thought I needed to find someone bigger who could help me to go further.

The Holy Spirit strongly convicted me that pride is birthed in that way. He reminded me that Samuel was not a king, yet he anointed two kings; Mary and Joseph didn't have a ministry, yet Jesus submitted to them; Eli wasn't a prophet, yet he helped Samuel to hear the voice of God. The Spirit of God told me that if I would die to my inflated ego and humble myself, He would increase my ministry and protect me in the process. From that time on, I decided to financially support my pastor—not as an act of bribery, but as an act of honor. My heart changed toward him, and our relationship has developed into a friendship. It's a practice that I will continue for as long as he is alive. I choose to honor my pastor because I want to walk closely with the Holy Spirit.

We are to team up with authority instead of fighting against them. Let's walk in partnership with our pastors and mentors. Honoring those in a position of authority reveals that we honor the Holy Spirit. Remember, we can't walk in authority if we rebel against authority.

Mission-Minded or Ambition-Driven?

When the Holy Spirit came upon Saul, he went to save a city. When the Holy Spirit left Saul, he went to save his title and fame. Ouch! God, the Father, gave us the Holy Spirit to enable us to fulfill Jesus's agenda to reach the world with the gospel, not to make us famous, rich, or well known.

But you shall receive power when the Holy Spirit has come upon you; and you shall be witnesses to Me in Jerusalem...and to the end of the earth.

(Acts 1:8)

Without the Holy Spirit, we get obsessed with titles, positions, and ranks. With the Holy Spirit, we care about His calling, purpose, and mission. Without the Holy Spirit, people are inwardly focused, needy for approval, entitled, easily offended, overly suspicious, extremely jealous, self-centered, living for the applause of man, ready to give up upon hearing the slightest criticism, and always blaming others. With the Holy Spirit, people heal the sick, cast out devils, save the lost, impact the world, and disregard what people say about them.

A Few Things to Keep in Mind

I am personally moved by King Saul and his dismal life story, which has provided me with many personal lessons on how *not* to live my life. I have revisited his story more times than I can count. Honestly, I observe in him some of my personal inclinations and temptations. By analyzing every detail in his life journal, I can see where my own story could end up if I take the Holy Spirit for granted and follow the path of compromise. Here are a few things that I keep in mind to help me stay on the right path with the Holy Spirit.

1. Pay the Price of Being Consistent

Saul started out well, but he didn't pay the price of staying true to his calling. He allowed pride to fill his heart and became self-sufficient.

> *And Samuel said to Saul, "You have done foolishly. You have not kept the commandment of the LORD your God, which He commanded you. For now the LORD would*

have established your kingdom over Israel forever. But
now your kingdom shall not continue.

(1 Samuel 13:13-14)

Passion must marry persistence in order for us to be consistent. That's why the writer of Hebrews told us to run the race with endurance.

Let us lay aside every weight, and the sin which so easily
ensnares us, and let us run with endurance the race that
is set before us.

(Hebrews 12:1)

Stay the course. Faithfully keep your devotional meeting time with God. Don't trade that precious communion with Him for anything. Keep praying, fasting, and sacrificing. Don't let your love for Him get shallow. Stay humble. Wait on the Lord. That was Saul's first big mistake: he didn't wait for Samuel. He went ahead of his spiritual leader and ignored his directions. As a result, God came and told him that he could not continue as king because he hadn't waited as instructed. God found someone better—not a better leader, better fighter, or even a better king, but a better man. What was so much better about this man that God found to replace Saul?

The LORD has sought for Himself a man after
His own heart.

(1 Samuel 13:14)

God found someone who was after His heart. Saul wasn't after God. It wasn't that Saul's sin was huge, but his passion for God was anemic—very shallow. David's qualification for the kingdom was that he always sought after God's heart. He stayed in touch with God, inquired of the LORD, praised the LORD, and feared the LORD. He was brave and zealous for righteousness. David wasn't perfect, but he was passionate. He pursued God with all his heart; he wasn't passive. Yes, David committed horrible sins, but he prayed not for the purpose of keeping the kingdom, but to have the Spirit of the Lord with him:

Do not take Your Holy Spirit from me.

(Psalm 51:11)

David always returned to God in repentance. He kept himself transparent before God, caring, and tenderhearted. And he respected those in authority over him.

If Saul would have sought God's Spirit as fanatically as he chased David, God would have shown him mercy. Instead, he was intensely preoccupied with chasing David, and therefore, God didn't let him catch David. If we stop chasing God, our pursuits will not yield fruit for His kingdom. Seek the Holy Spirit fervently. Follow Him. If you have failed Him, get up and cry out like David did, but don't let go of God. Go after His heart. You may not feel an immediate connection to His heart, but keep running after it. God is a rewarder of those who seek Him, and He will bless those who hunger for righteousness (Hebrews 11:6; Matthew 5:6). He is not looking for the perfect, but for the passionate.

2. *Remain Small in Your Eyes*

Samuel said:

*When you were little in your own eyes, were you not
head of the tribes of Israel? And did not the LORD
anoint you king over Israel?*

(1 Samuel 15:17)

Notice that phrase, "When you were little in your own eyes." When God anointed Saul, he was so small in his own eyes that he didn't see himself worthy to be a king, and he hid from the prophet who was sent to anoint him. But when title, fame, and wealth came, Saul became conceited with inflated self-worth. He became controlled by self and his hunger for God vanished. The LORD said in response:

*I greatly regret that I have set up Saul as king, for he has
turned back from following Me, and has not performed
My commandments... Saul went up to Carmel, and
indeed, he set up a monument for himself.*

(1 Samuel 15:11-12)

Your net worth should not determine your sense of self-worth. In other words, your title shouldn't increase your self-esteem. All of those things are gifts on loan from God, but you must stay humble, hungry, and holy before the Lord. When you're a nobody, God becomes everything. But when you become big in your own eyes, God becomes small in your heart. That's dangerous! Watch what you think about yourself.

I try to constantly remind myself where I came from. I like to say, "I'm a nobody trying to tell everybody about Somebody who can save anybody." Martin Luther said, "God made a man out of nothing, and as long as we are nothing, He can make something out of us."

Humility is not thinking less of yourself but thinking of yourself less. If you remain small in your own eyes, God will always be big in your heart. Be meek, modest, and humble. Stay hungry. Don't get so fascinated with serving God that you lose your fascination for God Himself. Make God your goal, not just a means to reach your goals.

3. Never Outgrow Your Need for Repentance

One thing Saul didn't apply to his spiritual life was repentance. He always made a bunch of excuses and blamed others, but he never repented. He apologized, hoping to get Samuel to honor him in front of people, but true repentance was never in his mind or plans. Apologizing to God is not enough if you're not willing to change. Pigs play in the mud and enjoy it; sheep cry if they get muddy. If you don't mind the mud, you are like a dirty pig. The Holy Spirit will not stay in that kind of dark, murky environment. Sin breaks the heart of God and it must break yours as well. Sin hurts God because sin is wicked and always hurts others whom God loves, including yourself. You must have a contrite, willing heart after you fail God.

Like Saul, I so often tend to seek relief instead of repentance. I want God to remove the pain and guilt rather than change my heart and remove sin at its root. I like saying, "I'm sorry, God," instead of, "Make me Your willing, obedient servant, Lord." I want God to remove the symptoms and/or consequences of my sin, not the sin itself. That grieves the Holy Spirit. He expects a turnaround on my part, with true repentance.

During his periods of demonic torment—God's signal to repent—Saul invited musicians to comfort and entertain him instead of inviting the prophet to deliver him. The demonized king sought sedation through entertainment instead of deliverance. He settled for relief instead of repentance. No wonder the Holy Spirit rejected him.

Pain and guilt can be compared to a blinking light on the dashboard of your car, which indicates there is a problem. It's foolish to ask an electrician to replace the light bulb in the dashboard instead of paying a mechanic to fix the problem in the car. Repentance is fixing the issue. Saul had moments of relief, but a lifetime of torment. He even prophesied at times when he wasn't following God. I urge you to never outgrow or ignore repentance. When I read David's Psalm 51 of repentance, I can see why God liked him so much. David didn't make excuses or blame anyone. He took ownership of his sin, cried, pleaded, and sought after God, the Mechanic who fixes people. Saul, on the other hand, made excuses and blamed others—his primary concern wasn't to seek God but to make sure he didn't lose his title and position.

There's no way you can remain in fellowship with the Holy Spirit without a humble, repentant heart. Remember, you may stumble and fail, but you can always come back to God's loving arms if you repent.

I've shared a lot about the Holy Spirit with you in this book and I hope your heart is stirred to get to know Him, to walk with Him, and to fellowship with Him in a deeper way. As I close, I want to emphasize one more time:

The communion of the Holy Spirit be with you all. Amen.
(2 Corinthians 13:14)

Blasphemy Against the Holy Spirit

When I was a teenager, I was bombarded with fearful thoughts that I might say something wrong about the Holy Spirit. Those thoughts were invasive and intense. They continued even though I was already a youth leader at that time. The enemy used my fear and ignorance concerning this topic of blasphemy to fill my mind with wrong thoughts; I feared that I would commit the one and only unforgivable sin. I did not know much about spiritual warfare at the time, nor did I have the understanding of the Holy Spirit that I have now, but I loved the Holy Spirit and I knew these fearful thoughts were not from Him.

There was a worry in the back of my mind that if I were to say something against the Holy Spirit, I would be condemned for all eternity. Maybe I had already committed the unpardonable sin. I was scared and lived in fear, making sure I did not say anything against the Holy Spirit. But after some time, those thoughts subsided and then disappeared. The more I've read the Bible, the more I've noticed how the devil plants that fear, and also how ignorance can play a huge role in empowering apprehension.

The number one thing I've learned is that you have to read what the Bible says in context. Read the chapter before and the chapter after for a broader perspective and understanding of the verse you're studying.

Therefore I say to you, every sin and blasphemy will be
forgiven men, but the blasphemy against the Spirit will
not be forgiven men. Anyone who speaks a word against
the Son of Man, it will be forgiven him; but whoever
speaks against the Holy Spirit, it will not be forgiven him,
either in this age or in the age to come.

(Matthew 12:31-32)

Why did Jesus talk about blasphemy against the Holy Spirit? The passage in Matthew 12:22-30 explains what happened before the verses concerning blasphemy; Jesus was healing a mute and blind man by casting a demon out of him. The Pharisees quickly jumped to conclusions, claiming that Jesus was casting out demons by the power of the devil. Jesus responded by saying that blasphemy against the Holy Spirit will not be forgiven! So within the context, we can understand that to blaspheme against the Holy Spirit is to give credit to the devil for those miracles performed in the name of Jesus through the power and authority of the Holy Spirit, especially exorcisms of evil spirits.

Because they said, "He has an unclean spirit."

(Mark 3:30)

We see a similar occurrence in the Gospel of Mark. The jealous Pharisees accused Jesus of casting out demons by the power of demons. They claimed that Jesus Christ was empowered by Beelzebub, who is the prince or ruler of the demon world. Jesus responded by saying that the devil was not having a civil war. The devil is organized, and the reason demons were being cast out is because the Holy Spirit was manifesting the kingdom of God on earth. Therefore, Jesus goes on to clearly explain that this is a precise example of blasphemy against the Holy Spirit.

So the topic of blasphemy was mentioned as a response to Jesus being called a devil for casting out a devil. A similar story is repeated in Luke 11 and 12. Here, the Pharisees did not say anything against the Holy Spirit. Instead, they credited exorcism and healing to the power of the devil when it was clearly done by the power of the Holy Spirit. If you take a closer look at the context, you will see that blasphemy against the Holy Spirit has very little to do with what we say against Him and more to do with what we say about His works.

If you are battling with thoughts or attacks in your mind that express anything against the Holy Spirit, let me share with you some comments that will help you overcome that battle.

1) **Focus more on the baptism of the Spirit than the blasphemy of the Spirit.** Living in fear of sinning against the Spirit is not God's will. The Holy Spirit does not come to live in you because you are sinless. Focus more on building your relationship with Him than living in fear of sinning against Him. As believers, we can sin against the Holy Spirit by limiting Him, grieving Him, quenching Him, resisting Him, or ignoring Him. The Holy Spirit knew that you would not be perfect when He came to live inside you. None of your faults,

mistakes, or even sins come as a surprise to Him. If you repent and turn back to Him, intimacy with Him will be restored.

Nowhere did Jesus tell His disciples to live in fear of sinning against the Spirit. Jesus told them to wait for the baptism—the full infilling of the Spirit. And we should do the same—live with the expectation of the Holy Spirit filling us, rather than us disappointing Him.

2) **Resist thoughts of blasphemy by speaking God's Word out loud.** The temptation to say something bad about the Holy Spirit can happen to anyone. Being tempted does not mean we have sinned. When we are tempted, we feel dirty and guilty. Jesus was tempted in every way possible, yet He did not sin. In fact, He was tempted to worship the devil. Yes, to bow down and worship Satan. That's an awful temptation. That tells me that being tempted with crazy stuff does not mean I am a sinner; it just means there is a bad devil.

Hebrews 4:15 says that Jesus was tempted in every way, even as we human beings are tempted. We don't see a physical devil speaking to us during times of temptation. He is a liar and deceiver and usually presents temptations at the level of the mind—our thoughts. Every sin starts in our minds. Yes, Jesus's temptation was in the area of thoughts, but His victory came through His mouth! Jesus did not fight the devil with thoughts or even with a prayer; He fought him with the Word of God. We must do the same! The best way to overcome temptations in our thoughts is through our mouths.

When the devil sends a thought to blaspheme the Spirit, just declare out loud that you love the Holy Spirit and that He is your Comforter, Guide, and best Friend. Shut down evil thoughts with your audible words. That is what happened to me as a teenager; I would verbally say the opposite when bad thoughts would come into my mind. *Let the weak say, "I am strong"* (Joel 3:10). When tempted, speak not what you feel, but what you know and believe.

3) **Avoid speaking against miracles, especially deliverances done by Christian ministers you do not like.** You might not agree with their style, method, or approach, but the Lord is using them. Differences are not deceptions; they are only differences. Some ministries cast out demons one way, and others operate differently. Some pray for the filling of the Spirit and people fall, but others don't do that. We have to be careful that we don't destroy each other because of our differences. We agree on the main things like the divinity of Jesus, the Trinity, the atonement, and salvation by grace. There are other issues, such as: Can people fall during prayer? Should we interrogate demons during deliverance? Should we have church service on Sunday or Saturday? Those things are minor.

If you attack ministries that move in supernatural power just because you don't have the ability to do so, you are probably jealous, and that grieves the Holy Spirit. It would be better for us to be students instead of experts in the areas in which we don't operate. Labeling people as heretics because we don't like what they wear, drive, or the way they live is dangerous. Saying that someone has the spirit of kundalini because people fall in their ministry is borderline blasphemy. Please be careful and don't just label things you don't understand as being the work of Satan.

4) **If you blasphemed the Holy Spirit in ignorance, there is mercy for you.** I know a lot of people who used to look at deliverance and say it's fake, it's demonic, and it's all staged, until manifestations happened to them or until their child needed deliverance. I have had parents repent for calling our church demonic when, not long after making those comments, their kids started to get demonic attacks. Those families would need help; so of course, we would pray for their situation. Usually, negative comments are made from a place of ignorance. We have all said something out of foolishness that was not pleasing to the Holy Spirit, but God is more merciful than we think.

Paul (a.k.a. Saul of Tarsus) rejected Christ and persecuted the church in ignorance and in unbelief.

> *Although I was formerly a blasphemer, a persecutor, and an insolent man; but I obtained mercy because I did it ignorantly in unbelief.*
> (1 Timothy 1:13)

Did you see the word "blasphemer" in there? Paul was one of those zealous, religious Pharisees who blasphemed, but after encountering Jesus, he admitted that he had no idea that what he had been doing was wrong. When God's grace opened his eyes, he repented and put his faith in Jesus Christ. Instead of remaining an apostate, he became an apostle. There is hope for you if you fall into the temptation of saying offensive things about the Holy Spirit out of ignorance or intrusive thoughts. I believe God's grace is bigger than our sin. We must repent and receive His mercy and go and sin no more.

In summary, all of this teaches me how sublime and how noble the Holy Spirit is. When you are living close to the Holy Spirit, you will not criticize revival because you will be a part of creating it.

Manifestations

*T*he Holy Spirit is not weird—people are. The Holy Spirit is unique and unrestrained. When He moves, power moves. When He shows up, anything can happen. All Christians love the Holy Spirit, but some are not comfortable with His unique manifestations. They reject manifestations that seem unusual, saying they are caused by demons. They think that if things are not conventional or customary, they cannot be from God. Dr. Michael Brown said, "You can have controversy without revival, but you can't have revival without controversy."[10] Why is that?

Well, the Holy Spirit is powerful and sovereign. He is God Almighty, and the Creator. In the Bible, a dove, fire, wind, oil, and water all symbolize the Holy Spirit. Note that these powerful forces can be both beneficial and destructive. Fire is not to play with; wind and water are uncontrollable. He is God; we are not. We are finite beings with mortal bodies. His power at times can cause surprises, such as

---

10 Giglio, Mike. "Leap of Faith." Charlotte Magazine, Charlotte Magazine, 1 Mar. 2008, www.charlottemagazine.com/leap-of-faith/.

Jacob being left with a limp for the rest of his life. After an encounter with God (Genesis 32:25), his walk was changed, and his hip was wrenched. Moses's face glowed brightly after meeting God on the mountain (Exodus 34:29). It was the divine glory of God radiating from his face. Paul fell to the ground (we don't know if he actually fell from a horse) and became blind after meeting Jesus (Acts 9:3-4). And let's not forget Ananias and Sapphira, who died because they lied to the Holy Spirit about their offering (Acts 5:1-11).

We are not even talking about people like the prophet Isaiah who walked barefoot and naked for three years in obedience to directions from the LORD (Isaiah 20:2-5). I wouldn't like to have him as a speaker at our church! Would our church classify him as a false prophet or perhaps a psycho? The prophet Ezekiel laid on his left side for 390 days and on his right side for 40 days, and cooked his food on a fire made of cow dung (Ezekiel 4:4-15). Their bizarre behaviors definitely top the lifestyle of John the Baptist who ate wild honey and locusts. The point I want to make is that most of us would be very uncomfortable around some of these men of God who demonstrated very odd behaviors. But God used them to write prophetic books of the Bible, which we hold in high regard.

Jesus Himself at times used some pretty strange methods of healing. He put His fingers in a deaf and mute man's ears and touched the man's tongue with spit (Mark 7:32-33), and he was instantly healed. Another time, Jesus made clay with His saliva and anointed a man's eyes (John 9:6).

Luke wrote in the book of Acts that God did unusual miracles through Paul, to the extent that people took articles of his clothing and put them on demonized and sick people. They saw God perform miracles as a result (Acts 19:11-20). That's not quite your normal healing and deliverance service!

But does that mean that everything that is weird must be God in action, or the crazier a manifestation is, the more God is being displayed? No. That thinking is as messed up as believing that anything unusual or unconventional is not from God. Let's look at some strange manifestations mentioned in the Bible and then we will take a look at a few tests we can apply.

1) **Falling under the power of God.** Some call this being "slain in the Spirit."

   After hearing the audible voice of God, the three disciples who were with Jesus on the Mount of Transfiguration *"fell on their faces and were greatly afraid"* (Matthew 17:6). I mean, who wouldn't fall to the ground after hearing God's voice resounding from heaven?

Likewise, the soldiers who came to arrest Jesus, after Jesus acknowledged who He was, *"drew back and fell to the ground"* (John 18:6). We don't know if they fell forward or backward, but they hit the ground.

As previously mentioned, Paul's encounter with Jesus was pretty dramatic: *"Suddenly a light shone around him from heaven. Then he fell to the ground"* (Acts 9:3-4).

Do you remember the beloved disciple John, who walked with Jesus for nearly three and a half years and leaned upon His chest hours before His crucifixion? There in exile, on the Isle of Patmos, John saw Jesus, not as He was on earth, but as He really is, *"And when I saw Him, I fell at His feet as dead"* (Revelation 1:17).

I'm all for God's overwhelming presence touching someone and them collapsing in total surrender, but that's different from a preacher who pushes them backward. That is definitely not the sensational glory of Holy Spirit power. I know it's cool in some circles to see people lying on the floor and others falling, but if God is not "slaying" them, don't push them. Period! Jesus didn't push people down, nor did the apostles. And we shouldn't either. I describe myself as a demon slayer, not a people slayer. My goal is not for people to fall under the power of the Holy Spirit, but instead, to see demonic chains, walls, and strongholds come crumbling down.

2) **Feeling of weightiness.** You may know that the Hebrew word for "glory" refers to the weight or heaviness of God. At the dedication of Solomon's temple, the glory of God filled the temple to the extent that the *"priests could not continue ministering because of the cloud"* (2 Chronicles 5:14). Later, the fire from heaven consumed the sacrifices and God filled the temple again with His glory. That time, *"the priests could not enter the house of the LORD, because the glory of the LORD had filled the LORD's house"* (2 Chronicles 7:2). God's glory was so real and tangible in the new temple that the priests couldn't do their duties.

I have experienced in my personal devotions, and in public gatherings as well, the strong manifest presence of the Lord, so much that my body felt weak and I couldn't stand. I would lie on the floor or kneel in reverence in the holy, awesome presence of God. Those precious moments when Jesus becomes so intimately real are priceless and unforgettable!

3) **Shaking.** Sometimes people experience the power of the Holy Spirit so much that they feel as though some kind of spiritual

electricity is going through their body and in response, their body starts shaking.

When the angel Gabriel, who was sent by God, approached Daniel, Daniel said, *"I was in a deep sleep with my face to the ground"* (Daniel 8:18). Another time, he described those with him, *"A great terror fell upon them, so that they fled to hide themselves"* (Daniel 10:7); while Daniel said, *"No strength remained in me; for my vigor was turned to frailty in me"* (Daniel 10:8). In Jeremiah 5:22, it's written: *"Do you not fear Me?"* says the LORD. *"Will you not tremble at My presence?"* When God descended on Mount Sinai, *"the whole mountain quaked greatly"* and the people trembled (Exodus 19:18, 20:18). Isaiah described his encounter with God this way: *"And the posts of the door were shaken by the voice of him who cried out"* (Isaiah 6:4). When the early disciples prayed, *"the place where they were assembled together was shaken"* (Acts 4:31). Jesus told us that at His second coming, *"the powers of the heavens will be shaken"* (Matthew 24:29).

God likes to shake things up at times:

> *Whose voice then shook the earth; but now He has promised, saying, "Yet once more I shake not only the earth, but also heaven."*
>
> **(Hebrews 12:26)**

Most of the shakings that I see in our ministry are demons trembling in response to the anointing of God. I can't say that every shaking is demonic, but when the shaking becomes violent, or a person begins to hiss like a snake, crawl like a snake, or bark like a dog, obviously these are demonic manifestations, not the gracious presence of the Holy Spirit.

4) **Holy laughter.** Sometimes a person may laugh uncontrollably under the influence of the Holy Spirit. First of all, we know that joy is a good thing! In fact, *"The joy of the LORD is your strength"* (Nehemiah 8:10). God is connected with joy because joy is a fruit of the Holy Spirit, as well as self-control (Galatians 5:22-23). The kingdom of God is about joy and peace everywhere (Romans 14:17). Jesus rejoiced in the Holy Spirit (Luke 10:21). The deeper meaning of that word "rejoiced" is to jump for joy and to be exceedingly glad. That's what Jesus experienced in the Holy Spirit. Wow! One of Jesus's disciples, Peter, wrote about us believers: *"you rejoice with joy inexpressible and full of glory"* (1 Peter 1:8).

Because holy laughter and laughing in the Spirit are not mentioned in Scripture, many people reject this as demonic or hysteria. Laughter in Scripture is at times portrayed in a negative light. Sarah laughing in disbelief was not seen as a positive thing. There are plenty of verses portraying laughter as a scornful response or mocking (Psalm 59:8; 80:6; Proverbs 1:26).

The first occasions of this holy laughter occurred during the Great Awakening revivals in the United States. John Wesley (in the 1700s) noticed this phenomenon at his meetings. He labeled it demonic right away; but later, after seeing the fruit of these manifestations, he changed his mind and acknowledged that it could be a result of the Holy Spirit.

But let's be honest; we don't see any mention of laughing when the Holy Spirit came upon the disciples or anywhere in the book of Acts. We read about tongues, prophecy, evangelism, but laughter is not mentioned. Personally, I have not experienced holy laughter, but I do know genuine Christian friends who have. I believe these people must be experiencing an overwhelming sense of joy, and even laughter, as a result of being filled with the Holy Spirit. Many of them testify of being free from depression or fear after those encounters. But I do have a problem when some folks make laughter to be their pursuit or focal point, or even a measuring stick for how much of the Holy Spirit they have by how loud they laugh and how much they roll on the floor. Later, we will look at some of the ways we can and should test manifestations.

5) **Drunk in the Spirit.** When the Holy Spirit fell on the disciples in the upper room, unusual things took place, such as the sound of a mighty wind from heaven, divided tongues coming on each one, and speaking in other languages. For the devout Jews attending the feasts in Jerusalem at the time, all of this was weird. Confused, amazed, marveled, and perplexed are the words Luke used to describe the reactions of those who witnessed these things (Acts 2:6-7, 12). Others mockingly said, *"They are full of new wine"* (Acts 2:13). As the Christ-followers were filled with the Holy Spirit and speaking in several different languages, the unbelieving spectators thought they were drunk with wine. The 120 disciples acted in such a way that the bystanders ridiculed them as being drunk.

Here are a few things to keep in mind: it was the scoffers and unbelievers who thought these disciples were drunk, saying they were intoxicated. Then Peter got up and started to preach: *"For these are not drunk, as you suppose, since it is only the third hour of the day"* (Acts 2:15). I want to note though, it wasn't the drunk behavior that attracted the crowd; it was that they heard the disciples speaking in their native language about the works of God. There was more to the disciples acting abnormally: there were tongues, fire, and a mighty wind.

And the greatest thing that happened was that Peter got up and started to preach the good news about Jesus as the way of salvation, and about repentance. The result was that 3,000 people were saved and added to the church that very same day. The focus wasn't on being drunk in the Spirit but on the preaching of the gospel and the salvation of souls.

I believe that being *drunk in the Spirit* is a genuine manifestation of the Holy Spirit; but often, people today abuse it by turning meetings into spiritual drinking parties. Remember, it was the world who said that the disciples were drunk and talked about what they had seen in terms of alcohol and spiritual intoxication—not the apostles. The presence of the Holy Spirit can be overwhelming and ecstatic, but really, the Holy Spirit came only to glorify Jesus and to convict souls of sin.

The true fruit of the Holy Spirit is a changed life, not tipsy, bizarre, and drunken behavior during prayer meetings. Even though the Holy Spirit is presented as living water, a dove, fire, and oil, He also brings joy as new wine. He is God. Preachers are not spiritual bartenders; they are proclaimers of the gospel; and the church is not a spiritual bar. The church is the body of Jesus, the building of Jesus, and the bride of Jesus. It's always about preaching the gospel for the salvation of people, not about weird behaviors, which only call attention to oneself. We welcome the manifestations of the Holy Spirit but must always remember the main purpose for Him sending forth His power: *"But you shall receive power when the Holy Spirit has come upon you; and you shall be witnesses to Me in Jerusalem, and in all Judea and Samaria, and to the end of the earth"* (Acts 1:8). The purpose and the goal are to be effective witnesses, not to have an experience of spiritual intoxication.

6) **Other manifestations.** These can include travailing and groaning under the weight of repentance or the burden of intercession (Luke 22:44; Romans 8:26). Or becoming speechless after an encounter, like Zacharias, even though he was made speechless as a discipline for his unbelief (Luke 1:20-22). Another event is falling into a trance as Peter did (Acts 10:10). Philip supernaturally traveled in the Spirit by being transported from one place to another (Acts 8:39-40). Paul experienced going into the third heaven (2 Corinthians 12:2-3).

Counterfeit manifestation: Kundalini spirit

There was a video that went viral where someone compared the manifestations of kundalini awakening to the manifestations that happen in Charismatic and Pentecostal churches. Therefore, some label any manifestations of falling, shaking, laughing, etc. as the kundalini spirit because of the similarities with kundalini awakening manifestations.

The word "kundalini" means coiled snake and is believed to be a divine energy necessary in the spiritual evolution of one's consciousness. It is believed that kundalini energy is the life force energy that lays at the base of the spine. As it moves from the base of the spine through each of the *chakras* (the word means "wheel" and refers to energy points in your body associated with different spiritual and emotional states of being), a person can experience an expanded state of consciousness and a feeling of oneness with the universe. The method of activating this energy is found in kundalini yoga. Kundalini yoga is the spiritual practice by which one channels this serpent energy up the spine to activate each chakra until it reaches the crown chakra, and you achieve enlightenment, or as they call it, "kundalini awakening." When people experience a kundalini awakening, many of them experience hallucinations, visions, body shaking, hysterical laughing, and other phenomena that they believe are manifestations of this energy.

But you must understand that you can't get kundalini manifestations without engaging in the specific spiritual discipline of willfully summoning this snake-like energy to enter your spine and nervous system. That is kundalini yoga. You won't get that by being in a worship service and praying to Jesus! New Age teaching and beliefs are at the foundation of those who pursue the kundalini awakening. Those beliefs are contrary to the gospel. Therefore, any manifestations that result from the false teaching of New Age and its practices are also demonic.

Now, just because some of the manifestations may look the same, it doesn't mean that it's kundalini. The devil is a copycat and a duplicator. For example, in Egypt, the magicians of Pharaoh were initially able to do the same signs that Moses was doing, but that didn't make Moses's signs demonic. The devil quoted the Bible to Jesus in the wilderness; it didn't make the Bible less trustworthy. There are false hundred-dollar bills that look like real hundred-dollar bills, but that doesn't mean we should throw away all hundred-dollar bills; it means we need to learn how to distinguish the fake from the real.

Below are three simple tests we should follow to determine whether or not manifestations are from God.

Testing the Spirits

Beloved, do not believe every spirit, but test the spirits,
whether they are of God; because many false prophets
have gone out into the world.

(1 John 4:1)

Even though this Scripture deals with spirits more than with manifestations, similar criteria will apply.

Is the gospel of Jesus Christ being preached? When fire, wind, tongues, and all the good stuff came on the day of Pentecost, Peter didn't focus on the manifestations, but on the message of the cross. Is there a message being preached or is everything all about manifestations? Manifestations must follow the message. What sort of message is being preached? About Jesus? Or about getting more drunk in the Spirit? Peter preached about the death, burial, and resurrection of Christ. We should imitate him. For example, look at the New Age doctrines such as reincarnation, the ability to become a god, the belief that humans are perfectly divine, Jesus was just an enlightened man, love is a state of consciousness, the Creator is an unknowable force, and that there are many ways to heaven. These are totally contrary to the teachings of the Bible, and therefore, the manifestations that result from these false beliefs are to be emphatically rejected.

Are lost souls being converted? Sometimes believers are enthusiastically pursuing only spiritual manifestations and no lost people are coming to salvation in their meetings. Their gatherings become just an insider club for those who want to go deeper into the spirit realm and are tired of the boring, predictable routines of the religious establishment. While I am all for fire, wind, and tongues, the whole purpose of the baptism in the Holy Spirit is for the world to be saved, not for believers to bask in so-called "Holy Spirit glory." If people aren't getting saved, then either we are totally neglecting the power to win souls to Jesus Christ, or those manifestations are not of the Holy Spirit.

Are lives being changed? Jesus said to judge a tree by its fruit, not by its size or its leaves (Matthew 7:17-19). Christ said that people will talk like Christians in the last days and even have prophecy, exorcism, and miracles, but no fruit of godliness clearly evident in their lives—*"You who practice lawlessness"* (Matthew 7:21-23). The fruit He wants to see is not perfection but progress toward holiness. Those who embrace manifestations but practice sin, raise a huge red flag. All genuine Christians struggle with sin, but we don't practice sinning or even tolerate it. If a person who is experiencing manifestations doesn't exhibit the fruit of the Holy Spirit, those manifestations are questionable. If a place where these manifestations are happening all the time has no desire or drive toward holiness, then something is wrong. You shall know the tree by its fruit.

We can learn from Jonathan Edwards, who, in 1741, wrote *The Distinguishing Marks of a Work of the Spirit of God.*[11] He asked five questions to help determine if it's a work of the Holy Spirit or not:

1) Does it bring honor to the Person of Jesus Christ?

2) Does it produce a greater hatred for sin and a greater love for righteousness?

3) Does it produce greater regard for Scripture?

4) Does it lead people to the truth?

---

11 New Wine Articles: God's Manifest Presence (no date) evanwiggs.com. Available at: http://www.evanwiggs.com/revival/manifest/man2.html.

5) Does it produce a greater love for God and man?

Yes, there are genuine manifestations of the Holy Spirit that may seem unusual to modern-day believers, but just because something is unusual doesn't mean it's demonic. Manifestations are not the goal; the message of the gospel to save the lost, which is the mission of the Holy Spirit, is our primary goal!

Speaking in Tongues

The gift of tongues was the most common spiritual gift in the New Testament church. All of the original 120 disciples at Pentecost spoke in tongues in the upper room. Today, there are more than 600 million Pentecostal/Charismatic believers worldwide—the second largest group of Christians after Catholics. Pentecostal and Charismatic churches are by no means a small, fringe movement; on the contrary, they form the fastest-growing religious movement in the world.

Yes, it's true we don't know for a fact whether Jesus did or did not speak in tongues, but every New Testament writer did. When the descendants of Noah didn't want to be scattered and decided to build a tower to reach the heavens, God came down and confused their language (Genesis 11:1-9). On the day of Pentecost, the Holy Spirit came down with a sound as of a rushing mighty wind and filled believers with fire, and they spoke in tongues (Acts 2:1-4). That same infilling still remains for believers today. Jesus Himself said those who believe *"will speak with new tongues"* (Mark 16:17).

Why do we need tongues? Isn't the English language enough? The English language, according to the Oxford English Dictionary, has around 171,146 words, but tongues weren't given to us to increase our number of words. They were given to deepen or intensify our prayer life and our devotion—our relationship with God. Tongues are an intimate and direct line of communication with God.

For he who speaks in a tongue does not speak to men
but to God, for no one understands him; however, in the
spirit he speaks mysteries.

(1 Corinthians 14:2)

When you pray in tongues, your spirit does the praying, not your mind, and you are not hampered by distracting thoughts or personal interests. When you pray in tongues, you declare God's wonders: *"We hear them speaking in our own tongues the wonderful works of God"* (Acts 2:11). So, tongues are not only for praying to God, but also to proclaim God's glorious acts in the spirit realm. We can also praise God by praying in tongues: *"For they heard them speak with tongues and magnify God"* (Acts 10:46). Paul mentioned that we can give thanks by praying in the spirit.

Otherwise, if you bless with the spirit, how will he who
occupies the place of the uninformed say "Amen" at your
giving of thanks, since he does not understand what you
say? For you indeed give thanks well, but the other is
not edified.

(1 Corinthians 14:16-17)

The most important benefit of praying in tongues is that we edify and strengthen ourselves. *"He who speaks in a tongue edifies himself, but he who prophesies edifies the church"* (1 Corinthians 14:4). And Jude also exhorted the believers:

> *But you, beloved, building yourselves up on your most holy faith, praying in the Holy Spirit.*
>
> **(Jude 20)**

There is a diversity of tongues. Tongues for our own edification are what we call our personal prayer language, which is directed to God only and no interpretation is needed. It's just a private one-on-one talk with God. Ask Him for an interpretation of what you pray in tongues in order to edify and build yourself up. Listen for what the Holy Spirit is saying while you're praying in your spirit to increase in understanding, encouragement, and inspiration.

But tongues for public edification are different; it's one of the nine gifts of the Holy Spirit that goes along with the gift of interpretation of tongues. This gift of tongues is different from the private prayer language because it's directed to people in a meeting, and it must be interpreted for their understanding and benefit.

How to receive the gift of speaking in tongues:

1) **Receive Jesus Christ as your Lord and Savior.** The Bible says, *"He that believeth…out of his belly shall flow rivers of living water"* (John 7:38 KJV). The prerequisite to this river flowing

out of you is your personal saving faith in Jesus Christ. It's important to understand that when you trust in Jesus and invite Him into your heart, you actually receive the Holy Spirit at that very moment. You invite Him into your life and He abides in you. When you speak in tongues, you release the Holy Spirit to speak through you. The verse above says, *"Out of his belly."* It doesn't say that this river will flow out from the throne of God. It flows out of your belly; out of your spirit; from your innermost being—where the Spirit of God lives. You don't need to speak in tongues to be saved; you need the blood of Jesus for that. You're saved through the gift of Jesus's grace. Once you are saved, you have this well (a river of living water) that wants to be released through your mouth. That river is the fullness of the Holy Spirit, and that flowing river is the Source of this precious gift from God called tongues.

2) **Just relax.** Seriously, relax. In other words, you need to surrender. Acts 2:2 shows us that the disciples were not striving. They were not struggling. It doesn't even say they were kneeling and praying—they were sitting. Sitting in a relaxed position. The Holy Spirit came upon them while they were sitting. Many times, when people pray for the infilling of the Holy Spirit with the evidence of speaking in tongues, they plead with God to give it to them. My friend, tongues is a gift. You don't receive this gift by striving or praying earnestly. The harder you try to achieve it, the more it'll escape you because it's a gift to be received—one that you release from your innermost being. Speaking in tongues is really the Holy Spirit (whom you already received at salvation) being released through you. It's not about striving for it; it's all about surrendering. Relax! Rest in His love for you, knowing that the Spirit of God is in

you. Rest! The river of living water is within you, waiting to be released to flow. It's no longer an issue about receiving the Holy Spirit but about releasing Him to speak with your tongue. Your mouth is the faucet and once you open it, just let it flow! When you understand that, it takes the pressure off of you. Your striving and begging are not necessary. The key is simply having a childlike faith and surrendering.

3) **Your will is involved.** God's Word gives us a few examples. Psalm 81:10 says, *"Open your mouth wide, and I will fill it."* Another passage says, *"They began to speak with other tongues, as the Spirit gave them utterance"* (Acts 2:4). It does not say that the Spirit spoke—it was they who did the speaking in tongues. The Lord is not going to force it upon you; He will not override your free will. This is not an issue of dominion or control because the Holy Spirit does not control believers. He gave you self-control. The Spirit leads you; He doesn't drive you. Everything that pertains to the Holy Spirit involves your choice. It'll have to be your choice to open your mouth and release the sounds. For example, if the city water line is connected to your house, you have water available, but it will not come out if the faucet is closed. In the same way, as a Christian, you already have the Holy Spirit, but your choice is involved in releasing Him. Anytime I want to get a drink of water at my house, I don't need to call the city utility company and request they send me water. No, it's up to me to just turn on the faucet. It's my decision how much water I want or don't want, or if I even want to use water at all. Many times, people say that if God wants them to have it, they will. No, it's up to you to turn on the faucet.

4) **It requires faith.** Everything with God requires faith. Hebrews 11:6 says, *"For he who comes to God must believe that He is, and that He is a rewarder of those who diligently seek Him."* Speaking in tongues is no different. It takes faith to trust that God will add meaning to the sounds you release as the Spirit of God fills your mouth with utterance. This reminds me of the story I heard about a little girl whose dad overheard her reciting the alphabet in her prayers. After several nights of this, the dad asked, "Why are you saying the alphabet when you're supposed to be praying?" The little girl responded and said, "I'm just giving God the letters, and I'm trusting God to rearrange them as He wants." It's the same with speaking in tongues; you release the sound by faith and God adds the meaning.

5) **Let go of the fear that the tongues you speak may not be from God.** So many people are afraid that what they are going to speak in tongues might be demonic. I want to clarify this point: the tongues you speak will come from you in the sense that you are the one who will begin to speak them, not some demon. Scripture clearly says, *"If you then, being evil, know how to give good gifts to your children, how much more will your heavenly Father give the Holy Spirit to those who ask Him!"* (Luke 11:13). Your heavenly Father is not going to give you a stone. He won't give you a demon and fill you with a demonic entity when you ask Him to fill you with the Holy Spirit. Jesus will baptize you in the Holy Spirit because you asked in faith. Trust in God the Father and in His unfailing Scriptures.

If you desire to speak in tongues, pray this:

Lord Jesus, fill me with Your Spirit. Lord Jesus, baptize me in Your Holy Spirit. Immerse me in Your presence and fill my mouth with Your words.

Begin to release the sounds that come, not from your mind, but from your spirit, and continue in prayer. It's that simple.

How to Get Saved

Believe on the Lord Jesus Christ, and you will be saved.

(Acts 16:31)

*B*efore you can believe in Jesus as your Savior, you must know what you need to be saved from. An umbrella saves you from getting wet. A helmet saves you from getting hurt. Jesus can save you from the punishment and the power of your sin.

Each one of us has sinned against God (Romans 3:23). Even if we try to be really good, we still fall short of God's perfect standard. We sin against God almost daily by not obeying His commands in the Bible, such as loving Him, honoring our parents, and telling the truth.

God is holy (perfect and separate from sin), and He will punish unbelieving sinners by separating them to a place of eternal death and torment called hell.

*For the wages of sin is death, but the gift of God is
eternal life in Christ Jesus our Lord.*

(Romans 6:23)

Due to God's great love, He sent His own Son, Jesus, to save us from this punishment by dying on the cross in our place. Then Jesus rose from the dead, proving His victory over sin and death.

*That if you confess with your mouth the Lord Jesus and
believe in your heart that God has raised Him from the
dead, you will be saved. For with the heart one believes
unto righteousness, and with the mouth confession is
made unto salvation.*

(Romans 10:9-10)

If you would like to receive Jesus Christ and His salvation, please pray this prayer:

*I come to You, Jesus, to give You my heart and my life.
I confess You as the Lord of my life, instead of myself.
I ask You to forgive me of my sins and make me clean.
I ask this because I believe You paid the price for every
wrongdoing and sin I've ever committed. I now receive
into my heart Your righteousness, and I declare that I am
saved and that I am Your child!*

Welcome to the family of God and your new life in Christ! Please let me know if you have just given your life to Jesus. Email me at hello@pastorvlad.org.

Other Books

Break Free
How to Get Free and Stay Free

Single, Ready to Mingle
God's Principles for Relating, Dating, and Mating

Fight Back
Moving from Deliverance to Dominion

Fast Forward
Accelerate Your Spiritual Life Through Fasting

Available everywhere books are sold in paperback, electronic, audio version. You can also download a free PDF on www.pastorvlad.org/books

Online Courses

*I*n 2020, Pastor Vlad launched online courses to impact the world by training up the laborers for God's harvest field. Many believers around the world don't have the time to go to Bible school or can't afford Bible training. Therefore, we make our online school completely free.

VladSchool consists of courses that are Spirit-filled, practical, and scriptural about powerful topics such as deliverance, the Holy Spirit, prayer, ministry, identity in Christ, etc. All of our classes are offered for free, thanks to the generous support of our partners.

Enroll today at www.vladschool.com to grow in the Lord and to be trained in ministry.

Stay Connected

facebook.com/vladhungrygen

twitter.com/vladhungrygen

instagram.com/vladhungrygen

youtube.com/vladimirsavchuk

www.pastorvlad.org

www.vladschool.com

If you have a testimony from reading this e-book, please email hello@pastorvlad.org

If you wish to post about this e-book on your social media, please use tag @vladhungrygen and use #pastorvlad hashtag.

Made in the USA
Monee, IL
15 February 2024

53502950R10111